A CAN OF
WORMS

A Collection of Stories and Poems by
Matthew McAllister

Tellwell Talent

www.tellwell.ca

ISBN

978-0-22881-242-5 (Hardcover)

978-0-22881-243-2 (Paperback)

Table of Contents

Acknowledgements

I would like to express my gratitude towards the people who have helped bring this project together in a way I never could have alone. First, my wife Olivia McAllister, who has provided creative advice for the manuscript, sketch concepts, and cover design. Kirsten McAllister did all the sketches, and helped extensively with the editing process. Lucas Penner also contributed invaluably to the editing. Don and Brenda MacBurney volunteered all the props for the cover photo. Thank you all so much for your talents, time, and letting me put worms on your plate!

You can tell a lot about a man by what he says you can tell a lot about a man by.

Don't Mind if I Do...

What have we here?

Some family
Tugged along by the tick tick tick
On Dad's wrist
Must have stuffed their sleeping bags
And loud children
Into the minivan
With frenzied quickness
For see here, on the picnic table
A skillet abandoned
Cast iron, heavy and not yet rust's haunt
A good find.

Drunkards are unwillingly kind
This morning: tire tracks—
Churned dirt can be followed into the clearing and
As lichens bandage the wound, I arrive.
Silent circle of new soot
Firecracker shrapnel
Smashed glass
Red spilled cups
Look!
Between two stones
Five silver shapes;
Five cans;
Five lonely and forgotten beers, for me
Fortunate loss
Of the reckless

Beneath the canopy
Spring is opening up like a jar of peaches
I am reaching my hand in—
Curled Ostrich Fern, sweet False Solomon's Seal, crisp Miner's Lettuce, Stinging Nettle
Perhaps this secret supermarket

Should better mark its prices...
Botanical thievery?
Name it as you will,
I'll return 'till the forests protest

At the credit union they are forgetting my face and name
I am forgetting my access codes and important numbers
These slow days come with a price
But I'll choose them again
And again
Until I fall off the face
Of this round and round,
This non-stop,
And against the better wisdom of financial advisors
I'll be glad

Memorable Men

To succeed, be keen
The man in your office—
What brand cigar rests in his teeth?
Are they expensive?
Inspect his chest and shoulders
For strength
Could he lift you by the throat?
Plan for it.

To succeed, wait
Wait for the going-out-of-business sale
When they're on their bleeding knees
And you're miles high
In your shiningest shoes.
Shake hands then.

To succeed, make believe
Jingle gold in your pockets
Reveal rabbits in your hat
Open tattered maps to Never Never Land
Fold them out of sight, quick
Raise your eyebrow

To succeed, mind your mouth
And your movement—
The lights click on
The stage is set
Captivated crowds crane closer
No hesitation
No asthma

To succeed, dazzle!
Crack mightily the sun and spill its light
Upon you.
Package paradise in polyethylene
Auction it for eleven ninety-five
But wait, deceptive you—
Buy them back
Heap them in the yard
Burn them.
We cling, befuddled
We cling for now

Quickly!
Time is leering
We're changing the channel
You need a finale
Smelt your gold down to a blade's edge—
With wild exaggeration,
With loud sounds,
Cut your grinning head off
Flourish it high!
We're spellbound,
We'll not forget;
You win forever.

Wedding

Three-tier cake
Tear-track face
Oh wedding
Oh wedding
As much a gown
As the funds allow
Oh wedding
Everyone shakes hands and stirs
But her shy secret admirer
This could all have been for him and her.
Wedding:
Toasts,
Laughter,
He drinks 'till he's filled up
Floats his feelings up and up,
Too buoyant
To stay down where he kept them.
Standing
And wobbling over to her
Wetly spitting out a few words
Detonating the room
With five fingers clenched
And thrown at the groom
Wedding,
Wedding.
Someone call the police for this
Because alcohol can steal a man
Someone call an ambulance
And someone pin him down
This little stucco church might never
See again the scene it's seeing now—
Wedding.

To Behold, To Marvel

What are your secrets, almond chocolate bar?
You entice with ease.
Artisans knew their work well
In devising you
Bravo

Somewhere, a symphony.
You are the sound of wordless feeling
You swell and ricochet in oscillating expanse
Until the energy is spent
And you tumble from the air.
You are craftsmanship and vigour
Many applaud

Seaside sunrise
You seize all my senses
You heave the tides into ancient rock until it bursts
Sombre red embers and purple splendour
Sand like silk
Indestructible pines grappling cracked stone bluffs
There is masterful vision
In your arrangement

This body I'm in
Forgiving reckless misuse with scab and repair
Comprehending the abstract nature of choice and of it,
Building electrical patterns
I inhabit you, even while understanding fails me
You are brilliance,
Though not my brilliance

But in this residence, in this human shape
Most baffling of all
Most marvellous
Is the gleam
The mirth
The plead
The uncouth celebration
The wild grief
The reaching out beyond myself to that which I recognize inside the being of another
So that when I say to it
"This tethering between us...
This shapeless tide...
This untarnished dreaming of your joy...

This, I think, is love"
Somehow,
It knows as well

She Savoured the Day

Porcelain teapot

Steamy aromas
On cool glass
Soften the sunrise

Cars on gravel
Going somewhere
Of no consequence.
Going elsewhere.

Here
Plum trees yawn,
Rustling
Mid-Spring's fragrant awakening
Hayfield greens
Potting soil
Through open windows
Aloft morning air

Between sips of pomegranate tea
You solve the mystery
Of the tablecloth's crescent stain
The colour of pomegranate tea—
Exclaiming aloud
To no one
Then teasing yourself for this
Like maybe your husband will
Tomorrow
If he catches you at it

Anticipations surface in whimsical shapes

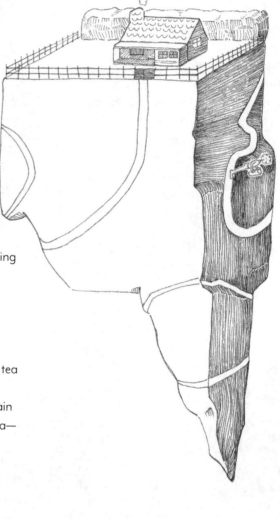

Slide your chair back
And stand
Cold tiles barefoot
Then sunlit warm ones
Where the cat sprawls
And cool again by the door

Garbage cans in hand
You strain and drag to the road for collection
Taking your time
Observing the small bird acrobatics
Your grandmother had enjoyed so much
Observing dragonflies'
Crinkling papery hover
Small things are life's sterling secrets
Small secrets best shared;
Tomorrow
He will be home

At the road
You lean to the fence and push your hair back
In strengthening sun
Paying little attention
To anything in particular,
Much like the weary truck driver
Early tomorrow
Changing lanes
Alongside your husband

Today you stretch your arms and brush the fence moss from your back
You turn to the house; you check the time
It is no countdown
It is eight twenty-four in the morning
The rest of the day will be lovely.

To Be Drought

Love throws itself from the ledge for its beloved,
I thought it easier on my aches to use the stairs
Love blazes aloud and exclaims of its treasure,
Small faltering placations are all that my tongue bears
Love offers up more than all that it owns,
I allot for this purpose a wage I deem fair
Shamelessly, love sends all else from the foreground;
With anxious sweating hands I hush endearment from the air
Love wars with the world to make safe its beloved,
I've faith in the munitions our attorney will prepare
Love harvests its bounty from the groves it has tended;
I lift high my hands, but the fruit is not there

Love cursedly perfect
Love longingly fierce
Love, you are foreign spoken language in my ears

A Shell

Not a husk
I'm not a shell
With a hearty sense of humour
With a centre full of vapour
For a soul
For a soul

Sail towards my island
And find only an atoll
The coral-crusted ridges
Of an empty ocean bowl

There is more!
Please and wait
I've a middle just like yours
It's the outside that is coarse
Somewhat cold
But the middle
In the middle
Still a glow
Still a glow

Hefty doors you've knocked and jarred
Windows found boarded and barred
Don't think I watch in disregard
I've thrown all of my weight at these things, and hurd...

Time
Piles
High
Months of footprints round this structure
Spiral outwards ever wider
Your siege engines
Worn and tired
You trail off to wander elsewhere

Wait...

Not a husk
I glow the same as you
From somewhere
In the middle
Not a tomb
And not in ruins
Not a ruin
You work inward
I'll work adjacent to you
We'll tunnel through
Tunnel through
I am here
In the middle
In the middle

...don't go

A Hilltop

From a hilltop
Watching the girl
Change a tire
Is less opposed
Than watching the girl
Change attire

Stars and Stripes (Sag) Forever

Oh joy
Oh me
Oh golly gee
The redcoats set their boats afloat
And left our brave country

Oh Jeffy
Oh Frankie
Oh, thank ye
You stood up and
Mucked out the cankerous manky
New flag flaps for freedom
So God bless the Yankee!

Let us sow and bloom anew
With time
Let us drink (a little) too
With time
Let our farm horse cede *himself* to glue
Let us sleep more
Let us sleep through

Awaken!
It's a new Red now
They profess to share,
But it all goes to Moscow
No curtain of iron
Will close over us
Wake up,
We must
We must!

But forty-six years
Is a long time to stand
Slow increasing ache
In the flag-bearing hand
Surely you're not at stake
Freedom, should we disband
Surely relax, we can.

To the white sands of Florida!
To roadhouses Nevada!
To the sensory smorgasbord sweet of the cinema!

To the one who puts this in my mouth,
Allegiance
To commander in chief, hip-hurray
Give him three chants
Of us, and that funny red light
In the houseplants

We won't bother with such details
For we're tenants!

Summer Evening

This park lawn
Summer stage music
We listen
We eat blueberries
Old acquaintances
New strangers
Inquire, perhaps
Chatter
Connect our heads?
Fragile exposure
We can try...
Trampoline shocks
Unfamiliar speech
Risk too great
Can't stay
Horizon beckons escape
No, feet: halt and wait!
Such something here in
The human, each
A cluster of worlds
To know them;
Wealth
I will subscribe
Let us span bridges between
Let us cross them and learn,
Invest me in each
To listen forever
Translate all your words into
Tactile canvas colourful
Knowable soul
Knowable to my own
But...
Tilting timbers
Thoughts mislabelled
Sales pitch

Boxes of poison
Squealing framework inconsistent
Rasping collapse
LIARS
You mislead!
You dare?
Your words molest
Both you and your liars who listen, nodding
Truths plucked and eviscerated
For favourable outcome
For glowing esteem
Drizzled in chocolate—
Easily received
...just please let me leave
I'll take me through the treeline
Hide away deep
In the moss
Where I know how to be
Where these humans are not
YOU, you are human the same

I know,

But if they feel this way
They conceal it too well
So tell me that's not how it is:
A thousand jars
With someone inside
And the lid on

Somewhere to Be Small

Earth that won't be torn and levelled
Trees who won't be tumbled down
        By iron teeth and wheezing diesel
Sanctuary here

Alpine virgin waters not to
Know the clamour of propeller
Trout leap out
Great birds dive in
Towering sky
The breath of wind
And sanctuary here

The air unsettled
Bending branches
Threatens every upright thing
And high above
Crawl blazing forks across
Grey underbellies;

Batteries
Of summer's sky
Of massive discharge

Fearsome majesty, and well prepared
To knock you from your feet
Should you strut unabashed, audacious
You, O' lightning rod
A good reminder
In the sky today:
You are no pinnacle.

Take cover, and take heed
For here (at last, relief?)
Learn how you needn't be

Trees and Benches

When I was in kindergarten
We had log cabin toys and a rice table
And an older kid died on the weekend.
After being sad awhile
The teachers planted a tree between the big school door
And my big favourite playground tower
For remembering.
Now the tree is big too
And those teachers work other places
And us kids left for high school and jobs.

When I was in high school
Math class was really quiet
And I joked out loud
About everyone being so quiet
And the teacher said
"Matt, someone died."
A kid in grade ten
I didn't know
I was in grade nine
I didn't know kids in grade ten
I didn't know what to say.

They built a bench for him
But really it was for kids to wait for the bus on
With his name on it.

If you sit on a bench
And sometimes if you look beneath trees at schools
You see metal cards with kids' names—
Remember, grass or weeds might be hiding them.
I guess the good thing to think when kids die
Is about the nice trees
And new benches

Maybe the good thing is
We might learn about what fleeting means.
Maybe if I get a bench
It will be where lots of very tired people are standing.

Something Afoot

Something is...wrong
It is in your inkwell
And my coat pocket,
The pattern of its boots track across strangers' faces

It is reclining in the penthouse
It is cursing and reeling in the basement
It is stealing bicycles and laughing in the alleyway
It is reproducing in the marrow of bones
And...something is wrong

It assures heartily
That nothing is wrong.
[Accidents happen!
Tragic and blameless exception
She's fine
Tell them, sugar; tell them *you're. Fine.*
Or you will hurt like a mother of—
That's my sweet girl.]

It is turning like a clock
It is setting like a trap
It has been found to turn a tidy profit
For some men

Words have been composed
To ward it away
But given time, words will sleep
And then it gathers them up
Melts them down
Into sharp and barbed things
[Delectable things]
Something
Is wrong

It is powder and shot to the East
It is needles and powder to the West
It is something,
It is reaching and taking

It waits in the champagne
Watching
Carbonation bubbles or devious eyes?

It makes friends quickly
Takes them home
And eats them slowly

Something looms close
[It is nothing;
Sleep.]

Brilliant Devil

Things aren't how I wish they were
Tall men subdue all the earth
Sharpened iron, tiny hands
Small farewell to innocence

Who can love the things we've done

What right have I to exist?
Beauty bent to wretchedness
Dinner repartee petite
Neighbour's house burns as we eat

Who can love what we've become

The world is not our pleasure vessel
Breached and in distress
The world's a shipwreck
Long since dashed and drowned
Ghost of goodwill on earth for fellow man
Dangling uncrowned
He's tethered to the foremast yard
Rotting rope 'round his mournful throat
His life, a casual discard
His sombre augur, anecdote

The bones of this earth are yours now, primal thirst
So have your way

Give us
Elapsing time,
Great weight of insecurity,
Slow obsoletion of empathy,
Sheer hunger for authority,
The yearning for delights yet to be
Lavished upon ourselves;
Give us, and see where we've been carried to today

hip hip hurray

Opening your fingers finds dark bullets in your palm
Consolation in the sight of penitence across waters calm
But with each paltry sulphurous blast
Stir trough and crest ever more vast
Until great swollen oceans that you dare not venture into
Culture in you long overdue woe begotten qualm

Still it's plainly now not crossable
And you've neither want nor will
Reform nearly impossible
You've neither want nor will

In the Wake of a Great Beast

The more I seek out beauty
The more I spy
Of lurid void and absence
Wherein beauty's since run dry

The more I fall down and implore my
Suspicions might be refuted
The more deconstructed life
I stumble through, aghast...muted

Then show yourself!
O' lumbering one,
Carving your swath
Shadowing the sun...
Who dares take what once flowed fully
Just to bleed it?
Who discards the breathless carcass
Once the thrill in it's receded?

I've still bills inside my wallet
I've still sinew, coursing blood
...I've strode past pleading impoverished
Treading lightly, as through mud

Therefore those who share in my shoes, if pious pride defeated
Could it be admitted then, at last
That we did?

~

Oh Lord,
I could understand it if you chose
To leave us to our undoing unheeded

Consoled

Fill your lungs with air
For you are loved
With love that kindles life in ashes

Let your fists be hands
To open up,
And grasp the one that reaches to you

Let this wreckage
Lift off from your
Chest to leave for good;
Now you don't have to hide in broken bricks
From scavengers
They're toothless in such
Sheer and boundless light

Bright morning's light
With words for you:

Though aftershocks still shudder,
Hold thee fast
Be joyful in this overwhelm
And share it.
Behold, your shadows vanish out of sight
For none of them can bear it

Sheer and boundless light,
Refuge
In you

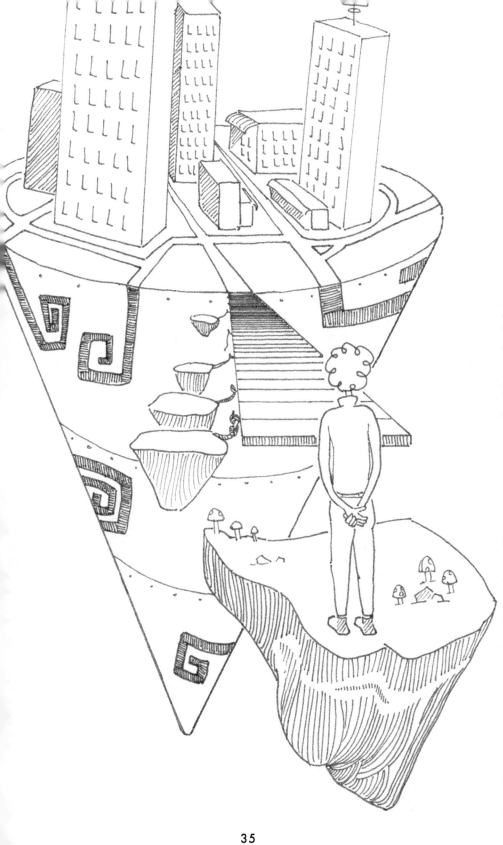

City's Shadow

They made wells in the buildings when they built them
Well-urinated stairs lead down
With locked doors at the bottom—
Not even moss will grow.
Dead leaves
And dead dreams blow in,
Collect

Here hunch the living remains of a man
Black welled eyes—
I don't know if he's been this way always.
He has about as many things to say
As cigarettes left
His favourite thing to do is rot...
He told me;
I asked.
Should I not have?

Grim collapse
Leads him by the hand.

Too often I walk in this place
Like fields of graves and perilous wells
Too much I fear I should fall in
And be swallowed

But today
Today I don't,
Today I leaped headlong, into it all
And breathed it through—
It was sweltering stench in all the ways I could know
But today I've a peculiar love for this place.
Unrequest granted,
Whooping plunge!
I want to listen
I want to swim in it
I want to sing with it
I hear its plea;
Staggering isolated, burdened heavy with the strong evil of glowering exile
Long years aloned in
Rot's garden

But life must strive with
Irrepressible hope
Hardship trampled so heavy...
Still
If there is green that can grow here today
Then let it be so
And let me partake
In the planting

Randy, Is That You?

Homeless Randy didn't wait for me,
HELLO?
Oh you can't skitter off now!
I'm in on tall tall tower street and the hungry buzzards
The buzzards are eyeballing *me*
Like double cheese fry spillings
Mind you!
If'n' I can
We'll surprise 'em
I'll chew on THEM
Yah, yah, youbet mmm
Bite right all their feathers right out
I'll pull their little bird tongues off
Keep it into my cola can
And my feet
My feet
They're...old now
I
ah,
nope

Yokels

What's for dinner tonight?
Bad crops
What's for dinner tonight?
Bad crops
Dad what's for dinner tonight?
Beetle meat and corn sprout rot tops

My strong dad he
Chop chop chops
Fifteen thousand feet of tall trees
Sorts the dirt out
Scrapes long furrows
Scatters sweet corn kernels.
Forehead wipe
And beaming huff, says
"Son, 'at's good enough."

We wait
We wait
Field's green fingers
Split the soil
Skyward stretching
Tender toil
Waiting, weeding, water

One day
Overhead: loud evil bird
Great Plains' nightmare
Swooping, gnarring
Spitting poison
Hunting stolen science
Hunting green undying fingers
For its monster men
Back home

Dad look!
Dad barks
Dad blam-kablams his shooting gun
Slow dad
Quick evil bird
Fell deed is done

Dial ding
Dad's desperate call
Senator, news anchor, constable
Pseudo-sympathetic shoulder shrugs
Yellowing fingers feed the bugs

Now,
Monster men sweat golden droplets
Feed them to pet geniuses
Scheme and scamper
Search and scrawl
Turn words to anything at all

Dad says his best
Words: cave man club
Smash Dad in face
Words snatch Dad's pants
His honour laughs
Dad lost the case

Dad, what's in the oven
For tonight?
Bad crops
Bad crops
Poison rotten roots
Overdue bills
And best yet
The fresh carcass of hopefulness
Soon as his old heart stops.
Dig in!

Coal Is Coal

The sun: immense and tireless, rousing the air, coaxing dead soil to life. For all that it has been attempted, no gadgetry of light or heat has been found to warm a chill in the bones quite like the early morning sun. Nothing reminds a man that the sorrow he may cling to need not burden him forever, quite like the glowing golden air of the early morning sun.

Kreg rarely experienced the sun—morning, or otherwise. If the sun had an antonym, people who gave such abstract concepts any amount of thought might consider it to be coal. Cold and deep and treacherous coal. In as much as it is easy to tell when a man spends his time in the sun, it is equally obvious when a man's days are down in the coal. Kreg hardly enjoyed abstract thoughts, but it was suspected that he genuinely liked coal.

Down deep, Monday morning through Saturday afternoon saw a ramshackle crew muttering and puttering about, excavating great cavities into hard black veins under the mountain. There was no mutter in Kreg. In its place, there was an ever-focused, patient precision. Not exceptional talent nor strength nor efficiency, but a certain expression smeared in the soot around his eyes: mild, amiable tenacity. Something which might knock the confidence out from under the feet of formidable opponents... or obstinate coal.

Kreg pulled the lever and blades spun. Chunks of black churned onto the collection belt. He smiled, satisfied.

It was Saturday. It was bright and the wind hurried low clouds along like stealing sheep. Andrea wanted it to be Thursday again. Thursday was when the girls would go out for drinks and laugh a lot and speak in hushed tones about exciting news and pretend to disapprove of men glancing often. Thursdays were fun.

She picked through the potato bin. Saturday was this. Saturday afternoon was potato soup for Kreg. Saturday evening would be soot and laundry and soot on her mouth when she kissed him coming home, and talking softly on the sofa about this and that.

Which was good, too; *today is good, too.*

She placed a number of coins in the old cashier's palm, then potatoes, onions, and a little wedge of cheese in her bag. *Today is good, too.* She made a tired smile to nobody and buttoned her coat up.

It was early Sunday. The air was warming and the dew was steaming and the steam was curling up and away. Leaves and helicopter seeds plinked against the closed window. Closed blinds hung behind it. Kreg sat at the table with enough light to read, and read.

The little brochure was bursting with bold fonts and exclamation points. "Something, something your own business. Something two-year course something." He sagged in his chair. Andrea had seen it in town and grabbed it for him. Their conversation had been short when she brought it up.

"Start a business?" he had said. "What business? I don't... I'm not anything much of a businessman, I don't think."

"That's why you do the course, silly," she had replied. Replied and taken his hand in an optimistic squeeze.

"I guess so. But then, the cost—all that money. You saw what it would cost to do the whole thing."

"Yes, I saw. But Kreg, it wouldn't take terribly long to save it up. Now with me working at the bank again. Remember it would pay itself off eventually, and most of all it would get you out of that horrid mine."

"The mine isn't so bad as they say you know."

"Of course, but—"

"And it's getting safer. Lawrence just brought in a brand-new air monitor machine and—"

"Of course but—"

"They've started to use some sort of frequency; they can tell what the rock is made of without even breaking it now. The stability, how much support we're going to need, everything. So really no need to worry at all, really. Last cave-in we had was... Gee, I can't even remember now. Ages. Ages ago." He had given his most assuring gesture and squeezed her hand back.

"I know."

Now he was turning the paper over. The telephone number was on the back. His head made a picture of himself, and then put a dress shirt on it. There was a big desk and, for some reason, a cigar. His figure smoked and signed papers until the image disappeared into billowing puffs. That probably wasn't even what business looked like. It was a world that, to Kreg, might as well exist at the bottom of the sea. He set the paper down. He heard Andrea get out of bed.

It was next Saturday evening—by far the busiest night of the week at The Stagger. For whatever reason, Big Earl always took it upon himself to show new employees "the ropes." He had so many ropes to show that it could take somebody weeks to untangle them all. Sometimes they didn't even bother. Eric was trying.

"...And so, m'boy, you need the feel. The feel and the smell. Ah yes! Even the smell. You learn your customer; your customer learns to love you. Take it from me, m'boy. Oh yes. When the customer loves you, the customer will buy—ohumoh-ho!—lots and lots of drinks from you! And so you need to know your town. Know your town and nobody's a surprise—you've seen one, you've seen 'em all! Take the coal diggers. Y'see, they come in Saturday mostly, and they take the whole place over sometimes, there's so many. And they almost always sit over there." He pointed a knobby finger towards several tables which seemed unbleachably darker than the rest.

"They sit there and hoot and yell and you can always convince them of whisky. But! You gotta hoot and yell with 'em, m'boy. That's the thing in it all. And tell 'em that the girls are looking over. Little nudge, little wink. And the girls! Always a few tables of girls around. And the girls... Do you have *the charm*, son?"

"Well I..."

"'Course you do! And let me tell you, with the girls, *charm* works like... Well, it works like...a charm!" At this he let out a laugh the size of seven or eight men full of seven or eight drinks. Drying his eyes with a sleeve, he plowed on.

"So the charm, the undergrounders, the girls, the snivellers...the snivellers! Yes, the sad ones. Tucked away in a corner most often, and let me tell you—they're dependable. This is their temple, and we fill them with the holy water if y'know what I mean. Thing is, you've gotta listen. Says he hates her with a passion, better be that you hate her too. Says he had a real job often enough and honest he just gambled for sport, then that's the truth. It's always the same, but you pretend it ain't 'cause they think it ain't, and then liquor 'em good. Funny thing, in my *keen observation—*" he brought up his finger knowingly, "it's most always those undergrounders with the troubles. Ask me why, I won't know. Ask me."

"Ah, why?" Eric recited

"Thing is...I don't know!" There was the laugh again. It could knock a person clear off his feet.

"Down in a hole all his life, I suppose. It's got to *affect* them if y'know what I mean. Any course, it happens like the coming of winter. Don't help 'em though; they don't want help. They want drinks!

"Now our businessman, he's a different game of ball. Different machine altogether. Tougher, yes a hair tougher, but," at this, Big Earl's face split a fault line of a smirk, "they're all pretty, pretty peacocks, with big green paper plumes for the plucking! You'll learn to handle 'em. You watch old Earl." He parted the thickening crowd like swamp grass and led Eric towards the evening's golden goose.

Big yellow leaves were landing on the parkland grass and the fresh-set flagstones, and in the little creek. There were so many that the creek was lost beneath, appearing itself to be a flow of leaves—slow moving, bunching and folding under, buckling like continental tectonics and tiny mountains.

To Andrea, who had ventured to cut through the park on her Thursday walk into town, it was a lot of nice and crunchy leaves with solid ground beneath. Like the step before and the step before, she stepped.

Surprise flooded into her little black shoes and up her calves. Andrea stiffened. Nerves and brain scrambled to sort out exactly what had happened. An understanding was reached and the cold water was identified as a small, bothersome puddle. In anticipation of dry ground, she stepped again. Her foot plunged again through deceptive leaves, and deeper. Frustration brewed up a few choice words. She raised and extended a leg in a tentative search for footing. Leaves atop water. Leaves atop water. Leaves atop exceptionally icy and knee-high water.

Sometimes, defeat reorganizes the mind in interesting ways. A small devious turn began its conquest across her scowled mouth.

With dwindling hesitation she splashed the foot down. She laughed and kicked. Leaves and water flew. "That's to you for my ruined shoes!"

Her flying foot carved out a wet swath of visible creek. The current pulled leaves to fill it, and Andrea slaughtered them upon arrival. The battle raged, blooming in her a fierce and unprecedented radiance. The leaves soon stood no chance. It was a massacre. She threw her arms up, triumphant, and then set off running and kicking and sloshing and splashing. Leaves flew; water flew. In a final spite, the buried creek bank tripped her up and tumbled her noisily onto the opposite shore.

Out across the field she stumbled, panting, regaining composure as the buildings neared. She would have to stop at Jennifer's to dry off before they went out. "It's a good thing Kreg wasn't here. He'd say I'm such a fool."

Kreg wiped his forehead and took off his sweater. He walked to the thermostat and turned it down. Andrea always liked it so warm, but she was out now with her friends, so down it went.

Thursday evenings were usually for cleaning. This Thursday was no exception. The hard hat, the belt, the wrenches, the headlamp—everything. "Miss a cleaning," he had always said, "and you'll miss two cleanings. Then three. And before you know it, your gear is blacker than Lobotomy Dave's."

Lobotomy Dave was nearly a celebrity figure down in the mines for at least two reasons. The first was an unusual divot in his forehead—a place you could fit a golf ball into. He maintained that he was born with it. Popular opinion was pretty sure that it was the result of nefarious experimentation— probably the government's, obviously failed.

The second was his imperious pride in filth itself. His boots and hard hat and every-thing between were greasy black objects shaped like boots and hard hats and betweens. Washing erased character, he'd often tell you.

Kreg erased the character from the lens of his lamp and gave a grin. Clean and serviceable for another week's work. It all went back into his pack and he checked the clock. Eight thirty-five. Andrea would be out for some time yet. He changed and climbed into bed. Morning would come early. He closed his eyes.

Andrea blinked. It was a big glass of colourful alcohols and syrups. Tropical fruit floated. A little umbrella peered suspiciously around for rain or intense sunlight, as any good umbrella ought. It was in the hands of someone shuffling his weight and wondering to himself: "What would Big Earl do now?"

"I know you didn't order it, ma'am. The thing is, it was ordered to you. Uhm, for you. By a man. By a—" His brain caught up and glazed the final attempt at *charm* with something actually somewhat charm-like.

"...By that man right over there, actually. With love. Actually."

Andrea's friends one by one withdrew from their conversations as they eyeballed the drink, and then the man over there, and then (with near synchronicity) Eric. Eric's volatile confidence plunged back into a sea of fumbling.

"So I'll just leave it here and you can... Well, maybe he'll come say hi, or maybe—I mean if that's the sort of—"

Out of nowhere, something named Earl towered up over Eric.

"M'boy, m'boy. We'll leave these young ladies to their beverages, and to their dashing strangers, and we'll go about our business. Business like the bathroom sinks—in screaming need of a clean, wouldn't you say?"

45

"I hadn't noti—"

"Good lad! You know where the rags are."

They disappeared around the corner. There was just the booth full of women, and the table sprawled with drinks—one standing high amongst them all.

"You'll at least go 'n talk to him Andri won't you?" This was Jennifer.

"Oh that would be... I don't really know if..."

"Andrii, it's not a problem...You *know* it's not a problem. Maybe he wants to ask if you'll do his...whatever thing...taxes!"

"You know very well that's not even what I—"

"Yes!" chimed Evelyn. "Go over, say hi. Hard to be worse than my... What was it again, Jenny? 'Speaseless rambling?'"

Jennifer set her most recently emptied glass on the tabletop.

"Yah, rambling! Maybe when you stop being on and on and on and about the kinds of dirts you feed to your inside house plants, I won't know for how your rambling... comes. From."

There was a silence.

Jennifer was a lovely person, sober. Andrea saw the remainder of the evening split off into two increasingly distinctive paths: one growing ever more enticing.

It was dark, as usual. There was a brighter tone to the tunnels that came with Friday and would be surpassed only by that of Saturday, especially if they shut down early. The crew and Kreg strode down the passage, past Lawrence's air monitor beacon flashing green for "safe," and took the left shaft. Conversation hummed and echoed, but Randy and Andrew's had taken over.

"Solar fuel? What, don't that have to come from the sun?"

"Sure, friend, but what's coal then, hmm?"

"Well it ain't nothin' to do with the sun. Coal's coal. Buried deep."

"Absolutely right. But remember, that coal came from somewhere. Friend, you have to believe me when I tell you that coal is just a lot of squished-down swamps and dinosaur forests."

"That's still nothing to do with..."

"And what made those swamps grow? Heh, friend you better believe me when I tell you it's our very own sun."

"Sure, sure, okay, but you can't say the sun gets stuck in the swamp plants all the way until it's coal."

"'Fraid I will though, in a manner of speaking. It's all in the particles. Particles and bonds. What makes the coal burn so hot? You're breaking up bonds. And what makes the bonds?"

"I know you'll say the sun. Not saying I believe it though."

"Friend, you have to believe it though. It's all science. Trapped-up sunlight buried deep. So now I say again (mark my words) if the boss would start writing things like 'solar fuel,' you know I'll just bet those protesting bastards would quit trying at their blockades."

"Ladies and gentlemen! Put your hands together and give it up for me, Dr. Andrew Simmons. Solving problems, solving everybody's problems! Hey, just don't ask about mine. Yessir, or have you heard the baaad news? My old lady (booo) did run off first chance she got. With who? The—heh!—the—ha ha!—the fat—hah! *Fat* ol' barber! Edgar himself!"

It wasn't Andrew; it was a Lobotomy Dave moment. There was the chorus of laughing, he got his coveted slaps on the back, then the excitement fizzled into awkward nothing and damp echoing footsteps.

"Sunlight," thought Kreg. He had never imagined it like that before. He arrived at his machine, brought the motor to life, and began his work.

It was eight in the morning. Kreg was already at work. Andrea stepped into her slippers and turned on the bathroom tap. Last night had been weird. The man she talked to was full of new words and shimmery glances and tales of the world. Geneva, Berlin, New York—they certainly sounded like intriguing places. Real style and everything moving all the time. Important people. *Real* important people. Her hands found the towel and she dried her face.

Probably you have no idea what to expect when you travel places like those.

The oven light was on. Strange. Oh, because the oven was still on—Kreg must have forgotten. She opened it to check out of habit, and saw there was a covered dish sitting inside. In it were...eggs. And toast and sausage. Keeping warm. On the counter was a smudgy paper: "Breakfast for you, eggs cooked right through like you like them, love."

Andrea slowly lifted out the plate. It was hot to touch. The room was hot. The room wasn't empty enough. Was there not enough air? Of course there was; the thought was absurd. Andrea tried to assemble her thoughts but the air was the problem. Or maybe she just needed to sit down. She was embarrassed at the small tear tracking down her cheek. She sat for some time, until eventually there was nothing to do but concede to hunger. She went to the drawer for a fork.

It was late Friday afternoon. The day was cool and blustery, and Kreg thought he would hurry into town to deposit his cheque. It would be only twenty minutes on the new trail shortcutting through the park.

Hands in his pockets, he felt a little fragment. He pulled it out. It shimmered glossy black in the unnatural daylight, so far from its deep native terrain.

"So you're full of sunlight, are you? I don't know how some people come up with these things. I would never hav—"

There was an unmistakable *shlop*. Kreg looked down. He was standing in leaves, and suddenly deeper than a moment ago. Cold creek water soaked through his boots. His mouth curled down. He sighed, "Perfect." He took another step and caught his foot on an unseen rock. His weight went forward and downward, sloshing him face first into fallen foliage and water.

Kreg would have expected his body to launch itself to his feet, cursing. It didn't. Kreg would have expected his evening was utterly ruined. It didn't feel to be. Black silt streamed out from within his clothing and disappeared under leaf jams. For the life of him he couldn't explain why, but when he pulled his head out, drenched and muddy, Kreg didn't get up. He sat in the slow water, a slow and insuppressible gleam taking hold of his face. In a burst, he flung up his hands and splashed backwards, all but his island of a face submerged skyward. The world sounded like great oceans. Lying flat in the shallow stream, leaf icebergs drifted above his neck and chest, nearly concealing him.

It was an unknown measure of time until frigid temperatures won mastery over his strange moment, but eventually Kreg thought it best to stand and depart this place. He rose to his feet. He walked dripping home. He chuckled to himself about how stupid he was going to feel explaining the wet clothes to Andrea.

It was quiet at The Stagger. Tuesdays didn't bring much of a crowd. There was an old couple collectively recalling the ages of their grandchildren. There was a dashing stranger rotating between sipping his drink, checking his watch, and adjusting his tie and collar. They were over a dozen times adjusted now, and he silently scolded himself for falling prey to his own nerves.

Every time! It was all the same problem. The whole reason his presentation had fallen so catastrophically apart was for the same damn... No, no. Not now. She would be through the doors in a minute and, what is a second impression without absolute composure?

He straightened his collar and pulled side to side on his tie. "You are a handsome devil! They've said that and it's true. They've said that *because* it's true!" Today would be blissful respite from the havoc that awaited him back at the firm. He sipped his drink. He swished the contents around and poised himself to radiate approachable sophistication. The doors did not open.

The chances of her running late one by one surrendered their percentages to the chances of her not coming at all. He glanced around the room. It was possible that everyone was watching. He could almost make out the things they were saying about him. Leaving... Would that be worse? And did she not enjoy his company only a few nights ago? And was he not a handsome devil?

"If y'd like my *humble* opinion, standing you up, sir, she's as fool as they come." A massive hand collided with his back in jarring sympathy. Professionally understanding eyes hunched down level with his.

"Lucky for you, you've got old Earl on yer side. Lucky for you!"

Artifact

The weight of objects
Like sponges to harbour scraps of memory
Away from the dissolving gale of time and forgetting
The weight of places
And scent in the air
Wrenching the body,
The exploding past

An Autumn

The leaves and the leaf rakes have declared their war
It's coffee and wool to keep the cold out
It's pumpkins and squash and impossible gourds
The weight of the clouds rattle gutters and drain spouts

We see our breath for the first time
And it curls through the rain
And more than a season is ended today

The street musicians elect hibernation
Crows chorus on over bus-stop bench hash browns
I had a whole plan but so little persuasion
And sometimes I think she was the other way around

So we stand in the leaf dams and little waterways
Knowing more than a season is ended today

Her city is alive in its rhythm
She sways around questions with unusual grace
I falter and I can't match step with them
Damned if I withdraw and damned if I chase

Sometimes trust perishes in a harrowing display
And so more than a season is ended today

I'd swear this city block once stood welcome and friendly
This oak tree we scaled above fall-breaking heather
These street lamps haven't always cast their shadows down in front of me
And the neighbours' faces darkened with the weather

So it's the walking through pumpkin vines frosted to grey
It's the shutting of the latch of the little garden gate
Some things that became in me here calcified to stay
The rest
Trickle through cupped fingers
Grain, by
Grain, by
Grain

Until no longer do I recall

Cope

Bricks are for hitting your friends on the head with
Houses are for stealing the bricks from the walls
So you'll find that the people in big brick houses
Make for the best friends of all
Let's stroll
Let's out—
no
no... Let's not now
Blue sky's watching
Sun's a spy
Not today
Not outside
Paint is for breathing if you don't like breathing
And putting paint on is for clowns and for war
And which one do you say you'd find the most frightening?
Frighten?
Nothing!
Heads are like eggs
Fried or scrambled?
Screech and scrape
Forks against frying pans
Today's escape:
Climb tree,
Shoot cans.
Sounds like doors painted closed
New coat
New coat
Criss-cross over cracks, much too much was exposed
Come back I'll hit you in the mouth I'll smash your teeth out!
Come back and say what you said and stand still...
...don't come back please leave alone the everything I think about
No more words from before, no nostalgia films
What noise were you?

Sweet and avid.
What noise are you?
Battery acid—
Out!
...out...

Blue Sky—
I'll be here
Hurling stones
Blue Sky will crack and collapse
Or will I
Under Blues Sky's tired tones

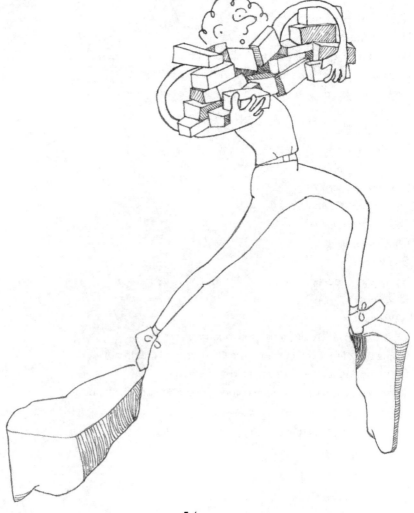

A Stone's Throw

Throw rocks at me
I think I heard
My voice
Declare me comfortable:
Sweating for leisure, not in toil
Dinner marinating in olive oil

Throw rocks at me
Toss sand in my face
Throw all my clothes away
I think I felt
My skin
Presume to warmth today
Then tonight swathed in down duvet

Throw me
Into cacti
Into a hornets' hive
Onto an eight-lane highway
I want to be sturdy and ready

Throw a ruthless punch—
The seedling grown in the greenhouse
May not survive the windows breaking
Invest in
Future onslaught!

So quench my thirst only
With the rains of a storm cell
Let me eat only
My own run-down gazelle
Grant me never
Whims wished to the wishing well
When I'm feeling unwell
And I beg to be suddenly sprightly and swell
Instead

Throw rocks at me
I want to be sturdy and ready
For the teeth of the world
When they come

Prairies Embrace

Today's sky hangs like over-ripened grapes
Moulding grey and ready to burst their
Great gushing musk
On tourist faces.
Summer's heat gropes it into bulging shapes
Summer's heat stuffs it with lightning power
Swimming air
Umbrellas swoon
Today's sky throbs heavy and kisses wetly down
Long tongue dragging tracks in the earth
Tiny tourists quailing

Speaking with Morris

"Environmentalist."
The word did not smell of regular hygiene
Or Morris...
It was probably coming from Morris.
Something about him
Leaped and begged for unrelenting critique
So I obliged.

It may have been the lengthy words
That he used in
Almost the right places.
It may have been his passive disapproval
Of most things.
Strangely,
He dreams of the same kind of world
That I do
Or I did,
Until he said it.

Morris,
You bastard.
You licked my spoon with your wet gross mouth
And now I can nearly see myself
In the morning mists of Cathedral Grove
With a chainsaw
With a dubious grin
Thinking of you.

Bliss

Rock-a-bye dear sweet
Close companions
Caffeine for weekdays
And beer on the weekends
And when the wind blows
It's no bother to us
[Calluses forming]
Rock-a-bye shake up
Don't close your eyes
Setting sun said I could...
Friend, those were lies.
Tonight it's the highway
No time, drive fast
Horizon; we'll be there
At last
At last

I'll draw you a picture
Of this time next year
Roast beef on the table
All assets secure
And if the wind blows
See that nothing will fall
See that no one need notice
A thing
At all...

Tomorrow Arrives

Here comes Tomorrow
He chews as he moves
And moves to the groove
Of vanishing youth
And the curse that he casts in his advancing path
Is a tranquil contented sedation

Here comes Tomorrow
Not inmate nor president
Nor discarded pocket lint
Could halt or make hesitant
His clockwork machinery mandibles
Churning agape for the sleeping and fallen

Here comes Tomorrow!
Your hurrying loved one tripped and fell
"Get to your feet!" was your dire impel
The sight of it all— intimate hell
As sobbing you curse, clamour, and plead
But she's gone
And she's gone

And here comes Tomorrow
The air rings like fire alarms and tumbling debris
The air drifts rank with sour blood and putrid mortality
The air hangs dark around you, dredging up depraved epiphany
Yawning jaws folding
Appetite enclosing

...here comes Tomorrow,
Delighted

With Shoes

I'm no major chord I'm diminished, lady
Blunders into ground wasps has been my lot, lately
The shoes upon my feet contend that I'm completely crazy

In many ways, it was hard to hear...but I appreciate their forthrightness.

We spend a lot of time together—
More than I and any other
Sew my sleeves and strap me in; they're probably correct

But who will mimic James Earl Jones?
Sing amelodic semitones?
Or drum percussion on their bones
And skin?
It's us!
Alone,
Again

So shoes and I will scale the cliffs
There from the top we'll spy
A hundred hundred thousand trees
All straining t'wards the sky.
So if such growth were gathered up,
Unto one single spruce applied

Great seismic Samuel Jackson!
Take ye stepettes backward!

What skyward rushing limbs unleashed
Beheld by human eyes!
Beheld by shoes, and I

Piracy

You've grown to an Olympian's stature
Collision with you will make strong men fracture
When caught on film
You're always the highlight,
In your company
The skies even are finite

Bronzing your skin in the sun—
Distinguished and daunting
Neglecting to acknowledge
Amidst audible flaunting

You've made towering things
Of the clay born to you
But born unto you it was

This proud song someone sings,
Though this proud song is you,
Has not rule over its singer's lungs

This song then, if it sours
Declining to unsour
To be singing this song grows unpleasing

And once entirely
Rancid autonomy
Might it wake to its melody suddenly ceasing?

Where the Forest Burned

Soot in the dirt
Soot encasing the trees
Lightning's blaze got hungry last year
And helped himself

Then melting winter left infant canyons
Gushing knives to cut easily naked clay cake,
But all have dried
And now I hunt thirsty, for water.

The worries out here
End almost with that—
That, and making sure
Not to mistake
Rounded leaf blade wild onions
For the sharper V of death camas.
Easy, really.

The onions are sulphurous spicy
The wind trembles silver aspen
There is room in the air
For thoughts;
No concrete to crash upon and break their necks
So what is next?

The people I love all
Live where everyone lives,
Where we scrub and clean
And scurry, anxious

The place I revere
Is right here
Where most things I touch
Blacken skin—
But worry not
And don't wash it off
Soot thwarts thirsty flies
And filters out black thoughts within

Here today
Two roads crest different horizons
Here today
Lies impossible decision

Regime

Valiant youth!
Drag before justice herself
The established order
And their trailing list of misdeeds.
Drive the old fools out!
Reset the table
Right the vessel
Uproot their garden of poison weeds.
Valiant youth—
Hurrah! Radical ecstatic today
Hurah, rigorous emphatic tomorrow
Ah...rattling static discontent, come so soon?
Now at the door we hear the demands of the
Vigorous new.

Change!
Of equal kind
As Paris fashion
And redecorated rooms

So what of the rally?
The forward push?
You brandish much smashing power
By only the rumbling grace of the clock
And the clock is known
To eat his children.

Therefore, turn me elsewhere
Seek me solid earth;
Unshifting in this kaleidoscopic ocean upheaval
Seek me the rock
That is

Sir, May I Have a Few Moments of Your Time to Share With...

Shined shoes
Sharp tie
Big black briefcase
At my door
Christ Jesus for sale
Get him while he's resurrected!
Free samples
Free pamphlets
At my door

Whose great-grandmother is going to buy in?
I see not earnest kinship in this suave apparel
I see not boisterous celebration cartwheeling good news down my driveway
I see in your hand a list of addresses,
Check marked until mine.
You don't look to be
Much like the words in your mouth;
You fit snugly into your particular corner of the world
Even while your generalities advise otherwise.
By all means your hand shook firm and your smiles are pleasant enough,
But the claims you stake are radical
And you, sir, are most inexcusably not radical.

Oh I don't know,
Who did I expect?
John the Baptist
Dishevelled and unkempt?
...It's just that you've cut small cubes from a glorious tree,
Brought them to my house,
Proffering them in place of the tree.

I do wonder:
If I'd not ventured the moss-clad limbs and magnificent canopy yet
Would I shoo you out,
You and all such associations,
With spit and jeer?

Simple

What do you do
On the unnamed hill?
Whistle cowboy songs
By now, you smell the part

What do you do
'Neath the weight of remembrance?
Greet the dawn, do your work, stoke the fire, fry beans, and ward the bugs off.

The Wind Stole Us

Now all the clothes fall off the trees
With red and bright luminous ease
Upon their banks the rivers feed
In storm they rise, in sun, recede

This great display
Is wrought of something
More than cutting winds
And churning clouds.
Such vista
Is merely where it dwells

It sings through branches, bends down grass
Now surging up in vast surpass
Of all us bound by weight and mass
All us who watch through window glass

And we are two
Who watch—
But imagine!
You and I
Granted participation;
Both our drowsy middles
Plunged through ice
Both yours and mine
Scooped up

Wind wound tight, then sprung
Powerless, we're flung

Through swiping twigs
And fern fronds soft
Through canopy
And now aloft
And faster yet
Up mountainside
Great granite fold
In earth's coarse hide

Diminishing foliage
Until gravel and ice
Reign on high

In timid trespass
We're set down
Upon sacred desolation

Shrill gale
Welcomes no visitor

Our feet imprint
Snow never trodden

Here, it is wealth to breathe

Historical Forks

Garret Bouchard had the greatest idea of his life. He thought and thought it over in the car, on his way home with groceries. Garret Bouchard got good groceries. There were burgundy apples, potatoes for roasting, two zesty lemons, pasta noodles with very Italian packaging, canned sauce with very nutritional promises, sugar-free yogurt, carrots, and an impromptu bag of BBQ chips, on sale.

"As soon as I get home, I will put this great idea to paper for safekeeping."

The light above the crosswalk was flashing for joggers. Pink and green jogging women bobbed across the road in the rain. Garret braked and rubbed chip remnants from around his mouth.

"So neon! Joggers are always excessive. No one will be running them over...accidentally. Oh look at the slow one, quite cold—shivering wet face, tight fists, noticeable nipples... Other girl in the green sleeves does long limber strides. Pink Top is huddling up her bare arms. I bet she hadn't even considered the rain clouds. Probably doesn't think much ahead. One of society's little blunderers—the type you're always waiting for, and finding her car keys for, and reminding her of everyone that she's asked you to remind her to call..."

Honking from behind reminded Garret that he was not moving and the crosswalk was now vacant. His flustered foot stamped the gas pedal and tipped the grocery bag on the back seat. Things rolled everywhere. He cursed a little, and then checked his mirror for scowling tailgaters, and then cursed again and assigned his embarrassed self to Pink Top's new blunder club, and then took some time to consider his life's adequate intellectual moments and moved the two of them together under a more forgiving "sometimes absent-minded," and then retraced his thoughts and suspended Pink Top's placement altogether for an inexcusable lack of conclusive information, and then scornfully repositioned himself among the blunderers for making such callous commentary, and then arrived home. It was almost dark.

Garret collected his goods from under the seats without incident. Garret unlocked his house and set the bag on the table. Garret contemplated eating the last of his BBQ chips, but opted instead to save them for tomorrow. Definitely this would have him back in his own good graces. He turned the stove on for spaghetti and put water and a coffee filter and coffee grounds in the coffee machine for coffee. He put the stereo on for a hip Gorillaz song that had been swinging in and out of his head all day. He smiled. He hum-mumbled along, stalking rhythmically and with heel spins in the kitchen.

Garret was happy and feeling glad, and soon had hot red pasta in a bowl, as well as a good enough mug of coffee in front of him. Tomorrow was payday at work; there would be significant overtime. The future was, more or less, coming on.

Later Garret brushed his teeth. He licked them side to side in the mirror and listened to the clean sound of it. He used his cellphone to send a good-night message to his girlfriend. He checked online for the tennis match results. They were favourable. The bed was refreshingly warm. Outside, the day's bustle was subsiding. Tire squeals and car snarls diminished like bad weather passing. He pulled the warm doughy blankets up and nestled into them. Garret Bouchard had the greatest sleep of his life.

Good People

Can we say that we know our minds?
We've so groomed and tamed our disposition.
Do the records note that we've shared sides
With the noble side upon social division?
Can we yet claim we are kind?
...Surely kind enough to dodge public derision

Are the trusting naive or innocent?
Are the innocent fodder for grand devious ambition?

Would you rally to the absence of what you aren't
Or the fabrics of what you are?
How can I know of these tangle-woven threads
Which to cleave from the others and cast away far?
Look here at these ones named Splendour and Honour
Cinched tight 'round the baneful red glory of war

Would you say it's for want that man takes,
Or the taking itself that he salivates for?

Can you know how the coward curses himself
In the burning dark between days?
Tear-streamed cheeks, pleading figures—
His orders, the trigger
Foul trench for the lifeless
Feral silent disgrace

Have you any words for him then,
That he doesn't yet silently, bitterly say?

So which of our juxtapositions
For the good, and a man like this
Recline upon more than favourable conditions
And the luxurious freedom from panicked self-preservation gone amiss?

Can merit be found in decision?
Or has goodness been always a gift

Anticipation

The coyotes yip excited when they've killed something
The candidate's elated when he's swaying the voting
Some men find delight within a fling
The same way
Twenty years ago
They felt about their
Turn upon the swing

My mother always likes it when the days get long
Trigger finger snipers wait in blinds and boredom,
Praying targets stand still in the throng

Gentle songbird writes one song
With her whole life
So does she have
A way to pass it on?
Or when the bird is gone
Is then her song withdrawn?

I want to be excited to be close to people
Ought we break through rooftops
With our hands and throw confetti?
For this life was given just to us
From nothing!
Let's get jubilant for everything that means—
Quick! I'll splash into the sea and swim straight to the Philippines,
Return with mangoes
Ripe and fragrant
Share in sweet and dripping smiling
All surrounding
Choruses of people all
Delighted to delight
In sharing word and song and humour
Good things, bright
Good things built

To dwarf once swollen evils
Now disarmed and insubstantial
Victorious us!

Every day, how is this not?
How dare we not?

Oh this life
I want not squandered
desperately;
The striving not to do so
Drags indefinitely

Angstman!

He says, "Give me reasons for rule books"
"Order," Dad's louring reply
Then a siren soars by
Towards alleyway cries
Oh, damn the timing! Quelling all compromise...

Wishes his name could be different
He wishes
To gouge himself out from
America's dream
His hair is the working man's standard
—Oh nauseous—
He's anxious to change it
The day that he's free

From Stalingrad's reincarnation
Suburban,
From dad and his bourbon
And chain-link control
This household's a match in a matchbox
He's certain
And dreams of the striking
To cremate them all

Now he says he'll put holes in his body
All over
And fill them with metal
To fly as his flags
He cherishes brash condemnation
He baits them—
Torching the scowlers
Like kerosene rags

Those hairbrush and handwriting idiots
Poor mother

With luck she might leap from
Her balcony ledge
This untasting world that they're building
Delusion
Swank succubus sales pitch
Rank bog, blind dredge

He says, "I'll never fall like they've fallen"
"Oh?" whispers some involuntary whim
"Do you not wear yourself
For the sake of yourself,
What separates you then from them?"

Your Valley and Boulders

You are a precarious person to be.
Many stones perch
Solitary atop many tall hills
All casting shadows upon
Your humble town
Down in the valley.

Carefree lives unfold below—
Paper and porcelain
In confidence
Of a tomorrow
Never visited
By the roll and crash of sorrow.

But you,
You forget them all
Atop the hills.
And why not?
Curiosity assures harmless
The nudging of barely balanced mass
Curiosity invents friendly mathematical estimations
Curiosity recounts falling stones of the past
Landing merely in brook and thicket.

You press your hand to it
Rough and groaning in eager sway.
You lean heavy forward and stiffen your arm—
Feet dig into dirt.

Down
And down and down,
The power of choice
Streams into kinetic energy
Lacerating the land.
The exhilaration of decision

Vanished.
In gathering clouds
Curiosity takes to her wings
And leaves you to new silence.
Crueller companions drift in with the mists
Whispering translucent maybes.

Only the long walk down awaits
And the fated news
Of your great cast die.

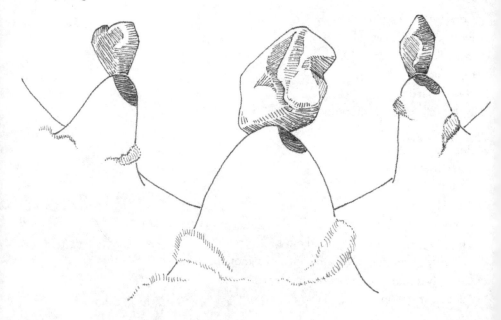

After Downpour

Aerial orange
Sunset severed storm
Begets bright magma in the road puddles.

And the green!
All the leaves of indomitable green
Smog and dust now scoured away,
They reinvent their colour.

Air still crackles
Cumulonimbus smoulder
Rinsed and new
Dark evening blue
Settles over
City streets

Brisk pedestrians
Eyes cast down and forward
Friend, I don't know you but look,
Share in this with me if—
Wait just... Sir
Ma'am?
Friend, is your head full of later?
...Share this with me,
We shan't have it again
Not exactly this!
One glance up
Too much?
Did you—
Okay...

Pasta

Love, I think, is like spaghetti
And I haven't a plate;
It's hard to keep from cooling off
But a mess to microwave

Tonight

I can be your seedlings trod on
You can be my tailings pond
It comes to this at last;
Tonight we're brazen.
I'll not ask my questions
In your molten gaze they perish
Wordless glance declared this harmless
Now draw near.
Mark an X beneath my neck
And root your blithesome fragrant vines there,
I'll sow mine beneath your stomach—might they grow?
It's so dark tonight I only feel you.
Something smoking, can you smell?
From in your skin
Billows billow, so
Teach me how to burn like tar
I'll tell you where my termites are—
It's so hot and dark tonight I only feel you
In your moving,
Do you hear the gnaw of tiny endless chewing?

For the Mirror

Ah, friend
Ahem
Yes,
Hello
Sorry! ...So sorry
Bad timing
—but
I've heard what has been happening,
Happening...*again*
Yes, yes—I am aware things have been rocky between us
But you remember, of course?
Your words?
You said, "Not *this* time,
Not *this* one"
You pleaded upon my shirt collar
With sentiments of... Let's see here, I'm sure I have them somewhere... Ah!
"Absolutely different than before"
"Special in a way I cannot explain"
And of course,
"Destined to *be*"
Wasn't that nice?
Fairy tale stuff is so fun
Now...humour me
Can you recall feelings?
Surely you must.
You were sky-high
On the pheromones of them
Walking (excuse my chuckling) into walls!

Where you supposed there ought to be doors.
Banged your face up something dreadful.

You invested
　　　...I said before...
Never invest

Evidently, you have not changed.
You merely move...as does the common snail
In apparent stillness.
You looked to have learned
—but...
(Pardon my weary sighs) upon closer inspection
You've been crawling upon your belly the entire time
feigning reform
Again.

My intellect brews for you many pearls even now
But, alas...
I fear they fall upon disconnected ears
So I will grant just this:

When you forget this inevitable sequence
Next year
I will have forewarned you
Just as last time
And this time
And when you disregard my helping words
Again
I will not stop
...Next time
...And every time
Because such is my regrettable duty
Whilst I am stuck in you.

Still Too Slow

Turning locks and closing curtains
I don't know how to know for certain
Hearsay flaunts her prickling doubt
TV says another city star is burning out
Out there
I think I might be unprepared

I'm not shadows
But how to leave them?
Ponder in the corner
Until worn and uneven
Hope is a strange thing
To claim to believe in
For somebody hanging
By threads frayed so frequent

So melting down the forks and saucepan
Take apart the stove exhaust fan
Strike and mould and form and fit
This metal can make me safe inside of it
Out there
Cannot always be unaware

But what a hindrance!
Heavy grinding iron limbs
Now what stifled
Metallic alterations grim
To outside sounds, all
Changed shapes and reverberation
Outside world still
Failed attempt communication
From here
Move too slow and disappear

Flickers and stir all around
But no faces
Flickers of sound
But I can't hear the voice in it
Movements quick
Movements abound
Increasing span of
Unoccupied ground

The flurry of life too nimble
But exposure's risk too severe
That vanishing dance in the distance
That ever elusive frontier

But Most of All

I want to walk trails ripe with savoury treasures
I want to be fruitful in ways outlasting my breath
I want to see weeping goodness avalanche through the dark hearts of all
Desperately I want one of these sandwich shops
To let me pee without purchasing their shit

The Cookie

You and I and everyone
Stuck firm in first person.
Who is our protagonist?
I am, of course
Every morning I awaken to my thoughts and senses
Every day they relay outside transmissions
You are intermittent
You exist while I perceive you
This life is evidently
The story of me

When there is one cookie left,
I will eat it
Because if I do not eat it,
The crumbling sweet
Doughy swallowing
Of the cookie
Will be lost to the unknown;
Potential sensory fiesta vanished
Into my nothing.

Or better yet,
I will *not* eat the cookie.
I will restrain myself
To crown my brow noble—
Challenge even the saints of old,
By such magnanimous gesture
As not eating the cookie
So that another might.

*   *   *

Was he commendable?
Was the act selfless?

Some would chorus, "Yes!
For look who was fed."

Others cry "No—a ruse
A flattery trap,
Game of invisible prizes,
Self-deniers, pretenders, performers
To be selfless
Is a mere shrewd trade
Of the physical
For social currency
And secret vanity."

It may be considered
That the ruse,
The error
Is much more a slippery little devil
Than either position
While at once inhabiting both.

It may be considered that selflessness in fact exists,
And dwells more humbly, down the lane and out of sight.

In all that were, all that will, and all now: a story.
The vast and twisted together tale of trillions—
Our protagonist's share cannot be assumed
Greater than yours or theirs
For any good reason.

He has assets: time, decision, ability
You as well have these.
Needs will arise,
In you or him or anyone
And the desire to apply oneself
To that which his assets most effectively improve
Regardless of himself

In this, it may be proposed
Resides selflessness.

For, why him?
Why should he be the fulcrum of his doings?
Is he the majority of life?
Does his pain and joy exist more absolutely than yours or theirs?
Can he stake any claim to significance that others cannot?
If no, then what delusion wins his being the favour of his decision?
Still, this is hard
This is not in our blood
In our blood swirls mutiny
This is paddling against satisfactory currents
Currents deformed towards one's imagined mass
Currents, it may be proposed, flowing from the unassuming headwaters of evil.

Scattered

They say set foot in every kind of shoe
Then you will stride
In confidence
And so she did

They say bridle your floodwaters and wildfires
Dance for rain and pile up fuel
Drink in their fury
Channel it
And so she did

They say to bathe in glue and run through
Haystacks and
Blowing pines
And salt mines
For then you will taste like something
So she did

They say persuade us that you love him
When you plead of how you love him
When you kiss him
In the kitchen
With the kitchen knife, then
When you heave it through his chest
You have to want to
With your gasping
And through perfect smearing tears
And with convulsions,
Hold our breaths

CUT,
Wrap

Decommission this one
Take coffee

She cultivates so many now
And they're as real as her
So many spools to wind back up
...Increasing crossover

She stands today like one upon
The pier whose cup was spilled
Into the waves droplet by drop
And wishes it refilled

Sam's Big Meal

Skinny Sam is begging for butter
Says "See me!
I'm bent and gaunt
Have pity please
Have pity, please."

Skinny Sam gets given what he asked for
Stuffs his cheeks
His stomach
His overcoat pockets
His arteries,
Grins greasy wide

Skinny Sam suffused in butter
Bent and gaunt so long
That he had
Only one thought in his head;
Eat
    Eat   Eat
     Eat   Eat
        Eat   Eat
       Eat

Protagonist, Troubled

Man with the steel-set jawline
Who gathered himself once
And straightened his spine
Liberated his languishing body of love for
The intoxicating warmth in distillery's brine
Yet harbours contempt for no one
Whom he leaves behind.
Promising champion for the good guys—
Training, promotion,
Now airdropped with semi-automatics
And a clever disguise
Behind enemy lines.
International conflict about to arise
Which he played
No role instigating,
Mourns deeply its perpetuating,
Every moment wishes he was staying
Home where the blackberry brambles
Sag heavy for harvest
Dogs fetch and are harmless
The small market's the furthest
He ever need travel at all
But alas, the call
Summoning his resolve
To someplace it is needed—
Distant justice impeded
Foes forcing his hesitant hand
To destroy

It robs him of life's joy
Once completed
Wants no place to be seated
To wave at the smiling lives he sustained
Above, blue sky
Stained

Below, among praises and cheer
He ambles away
For remorse
In evil's new exhilaration
In humans—
The cat and the rodent's corpse

Oh too much that was lost so to win
To win...

But most
The man with the steel-set jawline
Fears for after he's died
That his name and his deeds not be remembered
In sorrow,
But glorified.
For the boots of the butcher
And of the protector
Sit often side by side
Both suede brown and indistinguishable
Until after they're laced and in stride.

Omniscience Unfathomed

Can you smell the bitter smoke?
Do your dreams drift with mine through
Brick walls into rooms for
Unwilling surgeries?
Despairing pleads for pity and death
Observed, recorded
Animal eyes and utensils
Explore a bound and writhing playground

Can you hear the Zyklon B
Pull screams from children's trembling mouths?

I can't stop keeling over
Lord, with wretched sorries
Clasped to memories not mine
By words and stories

This with the dampening of distance
Years stacked become our barricade
Lord, but you
Where can you go
To be away?

How do you not rescind
Ours, a terrible free will
While it is chiselled sharp and swung by your beloved
To slaughter your beloved?

You, all places, you all times
Lord, you... How do you bear us?

Never Forget

Tomorrow is not mine at all.
It's yours;

You gave me today
So in silence, I'll listen
No more through my pinhole will I
Squint and name this earth your bad investment

Tomorrow's not riddled with holes
Like my old Gatling guns would have it
And come the day it is,
Should we fall through
You'll catch us—
Death and darkness empty threats

I hope!
I do believe
I do

Alive is wealth
Alive is to draw near to you
Alive is tempered in your remedy
Then,

Death and darkness
Chalk, glass
Pounce in ambush
Dashed to nothing

I hope
I do

Kinuseo

It is the most falling water I have ever seen
It is such surging immensity
That collision with the pool below
Detonates endlessly

White mist blast
Plumes up in the wind

Eyes closed, shoes off
Percussion underfoot
Willing me closer

Across rock faces slick and treacherous
The falling itself beckons,
Devouring the river above
Convulsing the pool below
Dwelling between—
An elusive beast
Ever enraged

I am astride it now
Soaking wet in ricochet droplets
One step further and we might shake hands
Two, and I'm consumed

I shield my face and gaze high
Peering into its great onslaught
Such graceful clamour
Ferocious rhythm I dare not join

Here is fear and beauty
Here is terrible good

Clod

Just a little bit quicker
And I could climb up the rain to the clouds
A little lighter on my feet
And I could stroll whimsically upon them
Then, with a little precision
I could puncture the sea in a five-mile dive
No splash
No sound

Not yet
Try it now, and I'd spiral down
Turbulent twist
Brine blast
Limp and sinking
Not yet,
Not even close.
I trip even on my shoelaces now
But soon,
I think

Wordhunt

Their population
Is dwindling.
This landscape crawled with them once
Each with a piece
Of something to say
And they would mate in the spring,
I would wait
To see what came of it.
A new crop:
Some slick and oily
Resinous heft
Some sharp
As chewed and unspooled aluminum accidents
Some very delightful
I remember
Desiring all of them.
So with snares
Grammatical bait
And rifle rounds
One by one they found places on my wall.
Proud grin I shone
A rosy inflammation
Such were the days
That fed me well
So today
In this vacant expanse
Where do they hide?
Have I taken them all?
Quarry exhausted...
No.
I will gather my things
And press inland
Surely elsewhere the harvest continues
Somewhere waiting
A new bounty

Honeycomb Sweet

Corrugated walls
To make tidy tiny spaces
Let us fill those spaces up
With each different thing we've captured

This one shouldn't speak to that one
Those few hide their heads and shudder
This one claims allergic to
Dandruff and dust and peanut butter

Turn the power out at night
Pull closed security dividers
Don't let anyone speak out
To unreliable outsiders

Extract and study
Study, learn
And then apply;
This is soon to make
Efficient everything

Ambition Becoming

Good morning, Northern Rain
I've driven through the night
With new windshield wiper blades
With many empty crates

Good morning, Ancient Air
I'm well prepared
Lungs inhaling, satellites tracking
Digital scales, financial backing

Good morning, Kings of Old
You stand so brittle
Coronet of lichen
And a robe of green dark needles
Let winds howl
Let trumpets sound
Now plunging hands
Through mossy ground

Good morning, Sacred Space
Are you not overjoyed?
This is my esteemed return
Unto our riches!

You were cool water, once
My steam-leak hissing heart valves
Took their refuge in your shroud
You were a place of providence
...Just as you will be now

Do you yield nothing!
Come, I've staked my future here
Coy, or unwilling?
Disclose, friend—
Have these dark skies and hard pacific winds
Swept away the secret warmth
You harboured in your hills?

I returned for *you*!
Embers from before still in my palms
Carried for miles
Returned for re-ignition;
To me, prosperity
For you, kinship and admiration
Great things!
Great things declined
Old bonds denied

Be warned
Great was my reliance on you
You, who let us down
How you have changed
Deformed before me
I thought you wise,
Now treachery
I thought you mine
Now insufferable silence
Fruitless roots of
Childish defiance

You must presume my will so weak,
I'm not the curdling wretch I was!
Today you're looking up the barrel of
Nothing more left to discuss

Fail to comply to me?
Oh, sweet one
You were ever mere commodity!
It was I, the fool, conceiving otherwise...
No more.

I pay men now to scour your skin—
They are practised,
They are strong.
They will find your heart
And dig it out

Smiling, old friend
Laughing
I will pay them for it.

On Wednesday Night

"Rubbish!" He flipped through the pages and let the book tumble out of his hands. "Atrocious. Utter rubbish—worse, a pussing sore upon the skin of modern literature. A malevolent plague sweeping far and..."

The visuals continued. Had anyone else been in the room, they would surely have been aware as to just what a disgrace this particular book was.

It was two hundred and seventy-nine pages long. Roses and a rusty lock made the cover art. Among it all hung the title, *Iron Keys*, in an obnoxious font. William hated obnoxious fonts. The author was Susan Benette, or as William preferred it, "sap-stuffed literary Antichrist Susan Benette, herself."

"Another vomitous masterpiece, courtesy of the one and only sap-stuffed literary Antichrist Susan Benette, herself. Hah! New York bestseller... Somebody go save New York." He picked the book back up and thumbed through it.

"Weak development, flat characters, plausibility? Not even a sniff! Of course, of course, she just *happens* to sit next to him for their fateful bus ride. By chance his life work *happens* to be the study of the glyphs in the cavern where they become trapped, and—" The book was flung to the floor with a sigh.

"Rubbish. Parasites do dwell among us, and they suckle upon the sweet milk of the imbecilic. We are overrun!"

William sat down at his desk and looked to the ancient metal typewriter in front of him. "What do you think, old friend? Do I go too far?" His hand clicked away at the keys. Tearing the emerging page, he read it silently.

"Hmm... Right you are, sensible machine. Yes. Yes and get to work I shall. They won't have decent works if decent writers spend their time choked upon sewage!" He crumpled the note, missed the wastebasket, picked up his pen, and began scratching away.

Nearly a minute into it, the phone rang. William cursed, set the pen down gingerly, and lifted the rattling thing.

"Hello?"

"Susan... Oh Susan! Oh...*Susan*. What's this for then?"

"Mmm, yes you said you would be."

"Yes, the convention. Can't quite imagine why..."

"Oh, nothing. Nothing! How did it go?"

"Yes, that's quite a lot of autographs, it sounds—"

"No, no, I haven't."

"Yes it sounds...euphoric."

"Your new book? Yes, I said I would, after all"

"Well, there were...segments that I...nearly enjoyed..."

"Example... Yes, well for example all of the words were spelled correctly, so you've clearly chosen a very sharp editor."

"No, well...no. Frankly I had a number of issues—"

"Yes, well to begin I found your dependence upon convenient abnormalities to be baffling. One could never expect so many moves of fate to fall into place like so; it isn't half believable. I can understand why a few might be fooled into overlooking such crevasses in the landscape, but surely... Susan? Hello? Mmm, I see."

William set the phone down. "Of course I never really expected a person of her variety to understand."

He returned his attention to the sprawl of papers in front of him. Finding his place, he took up the pen and opened a desk drawer, pulling from it a white die and a calculator.

"Now let's see here: a one and he makes the shot; a two, a three or a four, have a bystander take the bullet; five or six and no one is hurt. Right." He tossed the die. Three. An adjacent short and fat man was killed on the spot. William wrote it down.

He wrote for nearly a minute, then the lights went out.

"Damned hydro-electrical distractions! What is it now?" He rose from the chair and, with much feeling for furniture and the knocking over of his brandy, ended up in the kitchen. In a drawer he found the flashlight, and in the electrical panel he reset all the breakers. Nothing. The main breaker. Again, nothing.

"Double damned dysfunctional hydro-electrical distractions!"

The front door received a knock.

Knocking, as William theorized, is a better introduction than many realize. The crisp, evenly spaced three-knocks knock is employed by those eager to sell you something, those arriving in a dress shirt and tie, and those wishing to sound like someone in a dress shirt and tie who, in actuality, are wearing masks and gloves and brandishing a large crowbar. The rapid two-knock is that of a good friend you are expecting. The heavy and slow two-knock is that of a dreaded enemy you are expecting. The "woodpecker of absolute irritation" is usually earnest desperation. This knock was just such, so it was with little apprehension that William opened the door to this midnight visitor. He peered out.

Standing on the step was a wobbly and wincing man. He looked as if he had just lost terribly against some very superior opponent. William raised a woolly eyebrow.

Blood dripped onto the doormat. The fellow looked down, then up again. "Oh, sorry." William's eyebrows squished low in displeasure.

"I've been in a bit of a car crash, back there if you look, into the telephone pole. I'm not really... I can't really see much out of the left one and my head is—I mean my car is completely smashed. Could I call just for help just quick at your phone?"

William surveyed the dark countryside. The man wasn't lying. Sparks still erupted from a confusion of vehicle and electrical lines near where his long driveway intersected the lane. It was too dim to see much.

Curiosity compelled him to know why exactly this man was still alive, but he didn't ask. He instead used various adjectives to tell the man that, thanks to him, the phones were out and nobody would be calling anybody any time soon.

"Yes, right. Yes. No light on, no power on. I'm usually—I'm smarter than this. No power. I'll just will be walking up the road then." He turned to go in a stiff and clumsy pivot, like the hand of a dying clock. He was grimacing.

The sound of one's conscience clearing its throat pushed out through William. "You're going to hurt yourself, you know, if you go gallivanting in that state. The nearest neighbour is half a mile. They would call me inhuman for letting you do it... We'll—" He checked his watch. He glanced up at the man who was stopped and looking back. He rolled his eyes. "Yes, all right, fine. We'll take my car."

"To the hospital?"

"Hospital?" William leaned close and emptied his lungs into the man's face. "That smell like a drive all the way to the hospital?"

There was coffee and sourness, and underneath, sharp brandy.

"Smells like more telephone poles."

William grinned. "Next house with the lights on is my best offer." They walked and limped around to his car.

Coming out of the driveway, William's headlights illuminated the crash scene. "Incredible," he breathed. The hood was folded up like cloth. The passenger side was flattened completely. A fallen wooden pole lay where the back seat might still be. The driver's door was open. Inside were the driver's seat and steering wheel—neither with even a scratch. Ignoring the rest of the vehicle, one would never believe that it was incapable of driving. "The probability! Do you know what has happened here?"

"If you have to know, I was very distracted by a swooping petrel, which is funny because—"

"Not that, you daft. The probability! Pre-calculation, I estimate old death had three, four hundred thousand to one on you!"

"Hundred thousand? I'm alive—that's a one in one for me."

William wrinkled his face. One in one? He started to ruminate over this idea, but the appearance of a yellow porch light interrupted. They turned into the driveway meandering up and parked. The man opened his door and hauled himself out.

"Thanks, mister. It really would've been a long walk out here. Sorry, about your power. I'll call and get it all sorted. Good luck on the books."

"Yes, and, well, thank you, you broken branch of a man. Best of luck to you, as well. What the devil is a petrel?"

"A seabird. Which is funny because—"

"Never liked birds. Not even chicken—goodnight!"

William reached across and pulled closed the passenger door. The man chuckled uncertainly and made his way towards the lit porch. William put his car in reverse and backed up straight. The driveway made a sharp left turn. William's back tires sank into a soggy patch of topsoil. The house door opened hesitantly, paused, and then slammed shut. William cursed at the soil and stepped on the gas. The house door opened again, and a small pistol in a large hand beckoned the injured man to raise his arms and slowly walk inside. William didn't see it. Tires spun and he cursed the flora that had decomposed to become this patch of soil, as well as the weather system that had drenched it so. The house door opened again. A masked and housecoat-clad man strode out. He rapped his pistol on the car window. The face of William was creased and angry then flat and comprehending then white and horrified. As instructed, he turned his vehicle off and slowly climbed out. They proceeded inside.

Somewhere in an irrelevant cross-town location, a beige-white telephone was ringing. A mostly irrelevant beige-white and groggy man lifted it from the hook. "Yah?"

"Charlie?"

"Yah."

"It's me, Warren."

"Happy midnight, Warren. Good of you to call. Let's celebrate."

"Listen to me! Has anyone showed up at your place tonight?"

"Not even St. Nick. I'm disappointed."

"Charlie, you idiot, listen to me. You remember my old enemy? From the warehouse days? He showed up at my door half an hour ago. He even knocked. Like a little Girl Scout."

"He...What did he want to do, talk it over?"

"No. Or, I don't think so. He just stood there stupid with his mouth open. Was bleeding a little bit too."

"Sounds awful suspicious—you saying mine could make a move? I thought they didn't know where we lived."

"I don't know what I'm saying, I thought so too. Just, I don't know, keep an eye out."

"I don't think mine will show up. He's too old now. Plus he makes a lot of noise. I don't think he's ever up this late. I'll be fine. What are you going to do?"

"Do? My enemy is tied up in my house. I'm going to do what anybody would do. I'm going to find out why he came, and then I'm going to put an end to him."

William was studying the room. "Dingy," he said finally. "I dislike it. At first I liked it— antiquish and austere, with a rugged charm; simple and inviting. But it wore off. Actually, it's quite distasteful."

The man considered the room.

"Come to think of it," continued William, "does that sound like anyone I might know, or have recently met?" He turned his head sharply and with a deliberate effect which was all but lost in the grey dark air. "Some shabby individual requesting a favour—harmless? Oh yes, harmless. 'Let's take a drive to the house of my psychopathic friend. I hear he has a new revolver and some rope he can't wait to try out!'"

"Enemy." The man was straight-faced.

"Enemy?" William's mockery division loaded all its weapons.

"Not a friend. That man is my enemy. He probably can't even stand it, all his good fortune right now."

A short and airy laugh of disbelief escaped William. "Ene—yes, your enemy. Yes, people just have... You are saying that you simply shook his hand one day: 'Hello, good sir. Henceforth we are bitter foes, rivals to the end! May the best man expunge the other, mark set go!' Something like that, was it?"

The man opened his mouth to say something, but William's words overpowered and pushed it back in.

"And then! And then you maim yourself and tangle me into your doomed drift net. And then and then and then! And then we drive right up to the home of this...'enemy' and what do you say? 'Oh, um, good sir, William, perhaps we should try a different one—this particular residence contains a man intending to shoot me in his cellar!' No, no, not a word. This confounded slow-moving clown did stroll in and get us bound and impounded! I—" The fire exhausted itself. William slumped back into his corner of the room.

"Nobody knows where their enemy lives, 'else I'd of poisoned him years ago. It's just bad luck. Really...really bad...bad..." The man continued internally. William scratched at the wooden floor with his fingernail.

In the dark and the quiet, time seemed to clog and build and then break free and rush out— unconstrained by the rules one can hold it to by the power of the clock. It no longer moved in tidy intervals of seconds or minutes. Some time passed, but that was all that they knew. Then the door opened. The light came on.

There was a book titled *Beginner's Guide to Information Extraction*. It was in the hand of a familiar masked man. In his other hand were various sharp objects and bottles covered in hazard labels, and what looked to be a vice grip. William was troubled.

The enemy set everything down in a fumbling sort of way. He straightened up and walked slowly to William. "All right, old man. You're going to tell me what your deal is."

"I do not have a *deal*."

"No deal? Why are you parked in my driveway at one AM if you don't have a deal?"

William sighed. "Apparently...sheer, illogical, unfathomable coincidence."

"I don't believe you." He stood there for a second, and then turned and opened his book, and then flipped, and then read. Placing the book down, he hit William in the face. "You're going to start telling me the truth! Do you understand?"

The voice was much more threatening. Still recovering from the impact was William, on the floor, silent.

"Okay, okay. So it looks like we're going to have to play games. That's okay. Fine with me. I brought all the toys—let's play games. You like a little pain? You look like you do, old man. More to piss into those pages if I were so stupid to ever let you go?"

He sifted through his pile and pulled out a rusting, hook-shaped thing. He dug some more, and then more impatiently, and then stopped. There was a clenched and drawn-out "Shit." He thought for a second, then got up and left the room. Then returned, gathered up his "toys" and book, shut the door, and footsteps hurried down the hall. A car started and sped off.

It was quiet. William breathed. The man breathed. A little ant proceeded across the floor. They both watched in the yellow incandescent gloom.

"With any luck that's a fire ant," said William, calming himself down. "Waiting to sting fiery justice into this insufferable enemy of yours."

"Carpenter."

"Hmm?"

"It's a carpenter ant. They're harmless."

"How can you tell?"

The man shrugged. William moved his face around. "You're weird."

He looked about and up into the pitiful light bulb, pondering. "Has your little enemy club been spying on me by chance?"

The man looked puzzled. "Spying?"

"Yes, spying. You took me for an author—this brute alluded to it. I'm certainly no... no *Susan*, that much I know! Dangling such egocentricity before a stranger, at the drop of a hat. Not I! Yet, you both mentioned it..."

Some of the tension in the man's face melted into good humour. "Oh no. No, not spying. It's just pretty easy to tell."

"A certain charisma?" prompted William, scowl curving upward and lifting his brow with it.

"Um, no. It's...ah, nothing."

William waited, unsatisfied.

"It's really nothing. Not even worth... Oh, if it has to be something, look. There are all kinds of people who talk the way you do and all kinds of people who smell like liquor on Wednesday night, but there is really only one good guess about someone who is both of those things. Everyone knows that."

William couldn't muster the appropriate hostilities. "Ah, a reputation. We are a sharply defined few, that much I grant you."

Time crawled and leaped and crawled, again eluding measure. A car pulled into the driveway.

Tension returned. The man strained again at the knots holding him but with no success. Footsteps clunked and clomped down the old floorboards in a regrettably familiar way. The door handle turned.

It was either out of excitement, or out of his arms being full of even more, even more sinister-looking objects, that the enemy kicked open the door. He kicked rather hard. The ceiling made an odd sag. "I know how much you missed me, s—"

The ceiling sagged again, and then fell completely. The ceiling above the door fell, and the ceiling in the hallway fell, and the ceiling directly above the gloating enemy fell. Broken beams filled the room like spilled French fries. Ants swarmed out of the shattered wood, unable to comprehend the correlation between chewing through a thing and that thing falling to pieces.

William sat in his corner. The man sat in his corner. Dust coated them both. Nobody spoke for what may or may not have been a long time.

"This'll be a good day for you then. Make a decent novel or something, wouldn't you say?"

Sideways puffing, William tried to blow an ant from his cheek. "My good man, there lies the calamity of it all. As...*exhilarating* as such a tale might first appear, scorn and shame be upon any weasel who endorses it! I would sooner wither into utter insolvency than pen my name to such arrant implausibility."

Soon after, the police arrived.

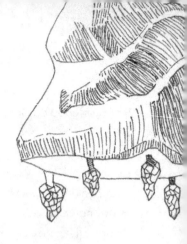

I am like Russula brevipes:
dense, common, and with a little depression in the middle.

Brain Fungi

Girl on street
Flowing dress
Legs and feet
Etc. Etc. Etc.
No time for that, for look at this—
Amongst the mulch and daffodils,
A nest

Sight above sights
Oh earthy smell
My mouth agape
My body swells
The heavenly huddled hideaway of
Hundreds of MORELS!

Oh yes

Oh no—

Morels...morels...morels
Thoughts will think of nothing else
Morels? Morels. Morels!
Caught me with their morel spells
My brain! My brain! Morels
They will not separate—

Please HELP!!

Modern Maiden

Something nice
Or something grievous
Just no more
Limbs live but leafless

That's the thing she's asking for

For gleaming sun
To warm within
Or cruel hard days
And tempered skin

That's the thing she's asking for

The nice looked like
A long ascent
Dreadful tugged
So down she went
A cut, a wound
Again, again
A bitter thirst
For discontent

Thus when rising tides invited inside
Found her
The surge was so much she could naught but
Flounder

Are They Peculiar?

Who goes to Subway tonight?
It could be anybody.

It could be teenagers, stealing napkins in poor stealth
To wipe clean their upholstery
From drunk Kenny's terrible moment.
It could be men in hair that's not their own
With moustaches,
With other people's wives.
Could be the estranged daughter of a sportscaster
Limited in choice of evening venue
By heavy rain and the prolific televisation of the big game.
It could be hundreds of rats
That operate
The skin of a man.
It could be tourists,
Could be nationalists,
Could be drug runners driving a seven million dollar van.

It could be only families
Who aren't at all absurd
Or bizarre;
It could be hungry people
enjoying a meal
Who watch the same films that I do—
Who believe that the world out there
Is as colourful
As I do...
We could be proving us all wrong.

Substantial People

The leatherflesh
The scar-studded iron-encrusted man
Grit and grind for breakfast cereal
Tolerant to an applaudable degree
Of heat
Pain
And alcohol
...Not born—
Cut out of a boulder!
Paid to strap the world to his back
And pull.
To avoid misrepresentation,
He is at the dealership
Buying massive horsepower that will make him so.

Shark's snappy eyes
Whippy word-whittling tongue
This man,
He finds his leather tanned black and stitched together
Custom tailored
To his blueprint body
Trimmed and tweezered religiously.
Metal is for wearing on chains
Oil is for hands and cheeks
In dry weather.
Heads will turn
According to plan.
Flash and dazzle!
They are all that one can hope to have,
So he is at the dealership
Buying sleek red that will make it so

Foolish me
Lacklustre
My vehicle says only
Check engine,
Change fluids,
Foolish me
Trickling through the background
Of substantial lives

Escapees

I can't hold this wriggling thought down
Was it urgent?
Was there a whole nest of them?
The answer...is yes!
But woe to me
They're hatching
Flapping
Swarming round my clumsy snatching
Up up
Past the moon
Look, even this one gone
Already
Goodbye small contemplation
I hope you were not needed

Being Alive (Spectator?)

The streets are full, right to the brim
But where is everybody?
Illusory distance plunges crevices
Between

Are they moving through tomorrow,
Sending expeditions forward?
Time restrains the mass but not the mind—
Launch forth consciousness!
Leave...only the receptionist behind
With learned words
For customers
For pleasantries

Or do they move not in the slightest?
Wrists and ankles bound in cord
Tethered to great steadfast stones
Of long ago
Stones heavier than current's churn
So separated from the wave of now
And all it carries

Are they like me?
Reaching for ripples
From the slosh and swirl of movement
By each marvellous and peculiar
Creature of disarray to pass
But in reaching, striking
Solid invisible
Like glass at the aquarium
Like train windows
Like a thousand miles
Until all drift softly off
Icebergs
Just dreams?

Like a Toy Boat in the Porcelain Whirl

I may not be your jazz musician
Nor ten thousand puzzle pieces begging for assembly
I will not be the Christmas goose stuffed with fistfuls of French sauce roasting in your oven
I will not be my own imagined fanatic
You take the sceptre— have it!
Oh don't you pen my shopping list...
I have no pant pockets,
I'll forget every word!
I can't soar in the wind; lunch was heavy gravel
Plink Plink Plink
Bye-bye, helicopter seeds
Spin free
I ought not to sleep like the winter
I declare!
I'll not again anchor my roots in the pebbles of treacherous ice-bound tundra terrain
Therefore, entertain!
Gumdrop grandma hawks boiled banana, takes tea, traipses across the savannah
Fancy that,
Next!
I don't want, I don't want...
That answer...I still know not!
Yet, parading forth
Dismissal, departure, dissociation
Hey, where did everybody go?
I can't comprehend lust for Las Vegas
I can't comprehend the physicist's eleven dimensions
(thus, he lies)
I will not enter romantic rivals' contention
I suspect chivalrous rivalry to be timeless cunning damsel's invention
I've since yesterday renounced all complacency
Now I cannot fathom this current complacent me
I cannot conceive why we cluster up
Like raindrops on slanted glass
As to fear what we can't overwhelm
...cowards

And I fear that I'm only the same
AmI? Iam. No,I... AmI?
Hush your narcicysts—
They'll ooze on us!
Don't you fear today might become nothing?
Do you fear to lodge love inside writing?
Fear in the thought that our
Twenty-nine thousand five hundred and three statistically allotted days
Will each slip by in menial ways?
I fear the contents of cigarette plumes
Fear the laws of Newton at great heights and great speed
Fear respiratory illness lurking in coughing
Fear slow submission to greed
I fear exiled habits should haunt me
I fear inclination towards anarchist's mirage
I fear to fear to become lonely
I still fear to operate power tools in Dad's garage
I fear great failings,
Fear all endings.

The Keys

Who carries the keys—
The will or the wilds?
How thin is the harmony spanning between?
By which one's decree
Do you honour and defile,
Cling to and dispel,
Nurture and ween?

The wilds rouse sheer and unsettling passion
The will raises rigorous witness cross-examination
They wait like the cold war
Drawing pistols at the train station
They tunnel ever deeper
To subvert the other's neural delegation

Who carries the keys—
The will or the wilds?
And how came they into possession?
Official trustee
Ceremonious transfer
Or alleyway quickfingers
Unseen and unquestioned?

Vern

He is turning fifty-two and owns a small refrigeration company out in the valley. He strives always to do work that he can be proud of. He likes the weight of manoeuvring money, but does not love it. He is trying hard to find his place in a world that does. He has been losing little battles for two years. Collecting payment feels like getting stuck in the elevator. When he owes, he pays—so why on earth won't they? This question is the sigh of many nights.

He has been losing little battles for two years. Debt is not so difficult to imagine as it was last autumn. He sleeps poorly when it rains. It rains often. He is an apparatus of ropes and levers—one of them frayed right through some time ago, and nothing has since been the same.

He is unreasonable when he is anxious. He knows it and feels full weight. His boiling moments dispel the respect of his tradesmen in slow sublimation; he catches glimpses, conversations drift through the shop when they forget he's around... If only a way to rearrange and fix everything! If only the ropes...

He is turning fifty-two and he owns a small refrigeration company in the valley. He dreams of the future, but not in the way he used to. Even his clothes weigh down. Did they always? His doctor is writing prescriptions and offering assurances. He quips phlegmatic humour and hopes to God that he appears composed. He sits in his truck and reads again the slip of paper. He turns the radio on to catch the traffic.

Stand at the Station to Miss the Train

Hands away!
There will be no
Pilfering of the neighbour's yard—
Vines and melons
Leafy green,
Scratch your head in wonder.

Take these tied together timbers
Which you call complete
And out to sea with you.
Maybe skies of blue
Will ever span above,
Cross tight your fingers.

Frailty is not how you fare
In lash and maul of hurricane's air
Frailty is the unaware
Who drinks and laughs and sleeps
When times are easy
Supposing how it is
Is how it will be...

How much, how much I wish that
This fatal frailty didn't fill me

Exclusion, PLEASE

The road less travelled is drawing a crowd
The side streets are filling up
Obscurity is fading into obscurity
Every hole in the mud
Has company

Because Main Street burst open
...They had to go somewhere
Because pressure is not in favour
Of closed spaces
Because people multiply and repel;
Foul association is anti-magnetic;
Hypocrisy external is a blaring siren;
Internal, hardly a whisper

Fat Orange Jeff swam in my lake
My lake turned orange
I *hate* orange!
Fat Orange Jeff can keep it
I depart for clear lakes remote
Lakes exclusive

Life Is

Life is a sandcastle:
Not yours—
Some little snot kid's.
He's smearing sunscreen on his tight shut eyelids
Stomp quick!
Whistle casual
Stroll aimless
Smirk
You are today's winner

*   *   *

Life is a bed and breakfast:
Appreciable enough
And toast is plentiful
But if you are crunching at the table,
Eyebrows raise.
Germanic innkeepers cough curtly—
With towering disapproval
You are shown the door.

Dropping the Shovel

Some ground works can be dug tomorrow
The sun rolls down the sky
Time spent to taste your lunch
And laugh
Cinches no noose
Pulls nothing apart

Waste is such a wry and crafty villain
But he's far removed
Today, so sit and stay
This won't
Punch holes
Or steal your steam

Stop trembling!
You nervous thing
And learn again what air can do
Besides turning the gears
That you've turned into

So be still
Inwards and out,
Now put the shovel down.

Great Extents

I'll break through bricks
I'll drink whole casks
You'd marvel at the strength of me
I'll fight with any brute who asks
You'd marvel at the strength of me
Your splinter fingers from the past—
They're all around and reaching
They have me by the ankle,
But!
I laugh

This face
Will ever laugh
I've taught it how to
Tell you nothing
It's a magazine written
To you
To keep you formless,
Keep you nothing

Now,
You warm not air
You fill no space

...So slip through every crack and draft
The splitting sidewalk
You seep through it
Wait and see! I'll pave it over
When the faucet drips
You're dripping in
But rags to stuff it shut (No drops to drink? So be it)
And when passing people turn to you
With phrase of yours
Or posturing
I'll call the squadron in
To rain down fire

You won't last
In my world
'Neath a crater!

Communicable

There's a lot I'm not
There's a lot I didn't
Warm wanton smiles misconstrue
Closing doors which
Crushed my fingers
Taught me to close doors on you

I did not desire to cause harm
But you tried to get inside
Have you not heard?
Nobody gets in
...Nobody.

Your face looks so familiar
I've worn those injuries before
We grow each day more similar;
Inflicted into inflictor.

Like some sadistic costly joke
Of endless cyclic bonds unbinding,
What shame feeblenesses invoke
To see plainly the spiral winding
And still set out upon it
In descent, and scarcely minding.

Her New Blanket

Yesterday
The air was bright blue
Depth unfathomable
Lily pad clouds slid east
Sun settled west
Night swelled
Night submerged our earth
Night subdued dawn

Early this morning
Dark grey dew
Drowned Sol
You can't see beyond the apple tree through the kitchen window

Sister,
One day you were running
And though you won not the races
You were moving
Cleft the air, and stirred the life in you
Your head, it looked to be
Bright blue
Clear and open
Summer thunder bursting
...but something fell on you

Something fell and knocked you down
Rippled through you
Silent conquest
Gave you greys
Gave you shakes and
Hangs above you

It takes more strength than you have sometimes
To master stairs,
Or breakfast

Struggles look like sleepwalks from afar
Sister, the sun's gaze was too much
You said
A blessed fog
Can soften piercing light
And shield the dread blue depth above
You say
It's chemical warfare
To stay awake
This is not the kind of battleground I've ever faintly known

The choice to
Narrow down your eyes
Unsheathe serrated steel
Tilt back your head
And bellow war cries out
To shake the planet
And your foe
Then run him through
This choice is denied you

How could you try?
Before winning the fight
To try to try—
What steeper odds against victory
Than irrepressible apathy?
I'd fight a hundred men three times my size
To never suffer
This fell thing assailing you

Sister, I don't know what to be
To fight on your side
But I want to
If it's a gale to cut through fog
Let it be so
If it's someone to sit and talk
Let it be so

I won't be another shake
That knocks you over
I'm on your side.
Would you help me find the way
To be on your side?

Kitsault

Weird little town in a far northern fjord
Hours from the world, built on miners' accord

Hospital vacant, the firehall's closed
White peeling houses, hedges uncomposed

Alder and thorn bush split sidewalks and sprout
Conquest began when the humans moved out

Dead summer drone of transformers...still on?
Trepid my step now, whose gaze might be drawn?

Sunlight betrays me, my footsteps invite
Listeners behind doors awaiting the night

Evening approaching, her shadows stretch long
Hastily striding, I do not belong

A brief pause as I cross back to gravel from asphalt,
What are you hiding, Kitsault?

Civilization, Great Success

Of harrowed cries and ringing steel
We've none
Of muddied hooves in unison
We've none
The rising, folding groan of serpent scales around the hull
Affect us not
For cities sunk and coastlines lost
The search
Is off

We've got the whole world
In our hands
We've got the whole world
In our hands
We've got the whole world
Felled and milled
And I'm so sorry

Monique on the Town

She is wearing her December skirt
In the blowing winter lineup for
DJ Raunch's Electronic Dance Night

Should she have a September skirt,
I would suspect it is very useful
In a case of emergency shoelace replacement
Or missing dental floss

Should she have a July skirt
I would be...
Surprised

Cynic Travels

Cynicism is a hard and heavy flagstone;
If you carry many,
You might pave for your stepping feet a road.
If it stretches far,
You might find yourself somewhere completely exciting.

But
Such onerous stonework
Before you arrive
May wear down
More than the skin of your palms and the spring in your step

I hope only that there is enough of you
Left of you
To make good of your labours
And time

You, the Harvest

Tractor-beam tongue here
Says you're the only one—
The only one there ever will be.
Is it true?
He pushes back wind-tossed hair and
The doubts you had
Align with his deep green eyes
And slip by slow slip they subside

Then there's faucet-face;
Wants to sweep you away
To some far distant place
With his socks and suitcase.
You considered suspicion
But his saline drips won
Purchasing your submission,
Disbelief overrun

Let them in, let them all

You see, you're the morning meadows
Cottonwoods and lilies fill
But eager minds survey your plains
Proposing their new lumber mill
Laying roads to soon inhabit you
Gauging your products' market value
Harvest you to grow illustrious and strong

Love like a coal mine
Love dressed up divine
Love for your love songs

Your Ocean Provoked

When the bait and hook bring nothing,
Then the wide drifting net.
When the net comes dripping empty,
Then drop down to dredge.
But take heed;
The slumbering depths
Are a stranger's playground
They're the surface of a different earth.
Who could know what you'll awaken?

Trees at Arms

January. All the bare branches in the backyard
Their long stick fingers scold
I'm leaning back and pouring gasoline in the firepit and
All over the Christmas tree.
I set the red can down.

Strike. Brandishing fire; fire is mine!
I could scorch them to cinders
With glug and sulphur stick wrist flick—
Be fearful, flora
Avert your knothole eyes
Bend away, skeletal twig towers!

Flame. Winter air is brief hot August
Green needles popcorn into ash
My new billowing friend dances over it
But he says this feast is full of water
Can't stay

Silence. Frost settles back among our poplars and alders.
Ceasing to cower,
They're looking

They're looking at this barely burned Christmas corpse
They're looking at the empty red can
They're looking closer and brawnier than usual

Absent?

Wake up with the springtime
Now it's not enough
Just to be just enough—
Things aren't so colourful
If they don't see the sunlight ever.
Stagnant air drips residue,
You lick your lips and
Wish for someone else's words
But they won't help you now
Too late, yes?

Wake up with the sunrise
Throw the pills away
And don't stay up tonight—
You thought you
Didn't have to think
Because you solved it in your head
Some years ago
And wrote it down
To file away
Inside that squealing cabinet drawer
You filled with plans
And locked
To never open now

Come, who have you been wearing
And what noise is in your mouth today?
The keys you hold but never turn
You ought not even have
Perhaps wings sprout
Upon your back
You haven't looked
And won't
Who are you wearing?
More than one?

Did you find them on the television?
And what would they say
Of this all?
Do imitations flatter
Or discredit and appall?

I may as well ask you
To give their answers
Now they live inside of you—
In your turn of phrase
In your humour
In your realigning social stances
Instead,
They are instead
They're your source now
They're instead of
Absent you,
Discarded you,
Of you, the friend I miss, who vanished.

A Questionable Sandwich

Exfoliation
If you stay long enough anywhere
There will be more of you
In the carpet and in the mattress
Than there is of you
In you
Exfoliation

Immortalized

Great winds bore the sky away
Some lamented
Bright lights overhead undid whole mountains
Grey fields are gravel
Fields cold below black air
And mourning stars

I wander weary
Maybe home is not in places
I, alone
Cursed to permanence
Blessed with wishes granted

People Who Walk into Schools

Grey shirt and a casual stroll
Stray words chip a gradual hole
The dam is groaning and the water is cold
Somebody should tell all the people below

Mind clings to reruns
Hands load machine guns
Throat croaking words, like
"I know she loved me once!"

It's a dark red ulcer on the surface of a soul
The six o'clock news said no chance at parole
Flags are half mast
On the channels we click past,
Saying
Some people
Find no way to mend
When they crack
Some people
Can't weather this world

Grasping

Take please this frigid water gathered up behind my wall
I'll cease to farm it for the voltages within.
It was such slow immensity
It overwhelmed eventually
You're the only one now with the breadth to bear its weight away from me

Grasp these hands in yours please they hold on for you
Straining tendons, slipping shoes
I don't defend my folly
Still, I beg beyond my dues
That you might set your hand upon me

All my efforts
Old ambitions
Draught to fill my head with power
What came then?
Each swirled away
Through fissures
To my curse and glower

Staggering, now
Naught to offer
A collapsing man fallen on his face
Hoping feverishly for
Unspeakable unrequitable grace

Hoping on
A whisper, long ago
Long held on to.
A whisper in the coldest plunge
Of incremental defeat—
Small boundless words from somewhere spoken once

"Truly, I love you"

Dead Barry

Barry is not real
I have devised him.
He lives in my scrawling ink,
But of course he could not know this.

Barry is five foot eight, has a bachelor of science, is himself a bachelor,
And will die of meningitis in Kenya,
None of which he can do a thing about.
Tragic tales are rich seams of humanity
I am their prospector.

I am Barry's writer,
Barry's chemist
Barry's divine.

I have penned the words;
I have done the deed.
Barry lies below shovels of bistre African earth
Set to traditional music
And the weeping of no one.

The piece is appreciable, and I flip to a new and empty page—
Closing the curtains on Barry's limited world.

The first incident
Took place during my Thursday morning coffee.
A draft through the hall and the whole house fluttered newspaper.
In puzzlement I follow the outside air
Into my study.

My wrath!
Oh, gasping
Some depraved delinquent has surely squeezed through the small window
Tearing from their bindings years of precious pages:
Pole-dancing Leanne,
William the melancholic novelist,
"Whisky first, family whenever"
And other such philosophies of Dale Kudd the drywaller...
Dead and scattered, all
Blowing irretrievably in the rush hour traffic of Forty-Second Avenue.

Depraved delinquent it was not.
In despairing autopsy, amidst naked and broken spines
There was a survivor:
The pages of Barry
Untouched

The fitful sleep of Thursday night
Ended too early.
Summoned to the doorbell, I was greeted with a peculiar parcel delivery.
Online purchase, rush air shipping, my own credit card number, invoice
"Paid in full."
Ampicillin Cefotaxime Ceftriaxone Gentamicin
Two hundred eighty bottles' treatment
Bacterial meningitis.

In the words of my dear Dale Kudd:
"Life is a stinking pan of piss. Pass the whisky."
The sleep of Friday morning and early afternoon
Was nearly not fitful at all.

The waking of Friday afternoon was terrifying.
A dry and papery mouth sensation pushed through
Heavy inebriation.
Eyelids parting did not reveal my living room ceiling—rather, darkness.
My limbs scrambled me up
With a choked yowl.
Scaly dry sliding sounds surrounded
I rose out of the heap,
An innumerable mass of white blank paper
Looming like evil snow
Over floor and furniture, up to my knees.

From my mouth I spat one single crumpled leaf.
It was immediately recognized,
However—much of my writing
On this final page of the life of Barry,
Was scratched through vindictively
With alterations scribbled above:

"Barry's head ached with the throb of **hangovers from his hot tub party last night. All
the women were kissing him!**"
"He soon descended into **the store for lucky lottery tickets and then he won eighty
million shillings damn straight YES!**"
"Were he **not** alive for the **somebody else's** funeral, he might **not** have enjoyed the
appropriateness of his own name, as scoops of earth **will be stuffed down the fucking
throat of this fucker who fucking contrived my fucking life!!**"

What to say,
My feet shuffled noisily
What to say...
I asked aloud if the changes had worked
No reply.
I asked how could he have located me
No reply.

Suddenly the four legs of my applewood desk screeched and skittered across the floor
In a wake of white
Towards me.
It ground to a halt.
Upon it were two items:
A stack of crisp new paper,
The top sheet titled *"**Part Two—Paradise Afterlife**,"*
And a pen.

From nowhere, a handful of
Bistre earth
Sprinkled definitively upon my desktop.
From somewhere very close
Malignant smiling.

Glossary of Non-Existent Terms

Shiningest: Proportionally related to "shining" as "shiniest" is to "shiny." Whereas "shiniest" describes an attribute of the object, which may or may not be observable at the time of reference, depending upon environmental conditions, "shiningest" describes the very action of shining (the most.)

Stepettes: Very small, hurried steps—often in reaction to some sudden danger. A startled movement of self-preservation.

Leatherflesh: An exceptionally durable and impervious person; used both in reference to physical attributes and temperament.

Narcicyst: A self-absorbed tendency repugnant in nature.

Quickfingers: A thief; a pickpocket.

CPSIA information can be obtained
at www.ICGtesting.com
Printed in the USA
LVHW081924291019
635761LV00001B/1/P